Lifelong Learning and Higher Education

SECOND EDITION

Lifelong Learning and Higher Education

SECOND EDITION

CHRISTOPHER K KNAPPER
ARTHUR J CROPLEY

KOGAN
PAGE

First published in 1985 by Croom Helm
This second edition published in 1991 by Kogan Page

Kogan Page Limited
120 Pentonville Road
London N1 9JN

British Library Cataloguing in Publication Data

A CIP record for this book is available from the
British Library.

ISBN 07494 0297 0

Typeset by DP Photosetting, Aylesbury, Bucks
Printed and bound in Great Britain by
Biddles Ltd, Guildford and Kings Lynn

Contents

Preface to the second edition

Since the first edition of this book appeared in 1985 the world has seen some major political changes. Developments in Europe seem to hold out prospects for an end to the arms race and the possibility of a new era of international cooperation. But the planet continues to face formidable problems, notably those of protecting the environment, controlling population growth and coping with severe human deprivation in many parts of the world. These are not just political issues, but also provide a formidable educational challenge.

Higher education institutions are still groping for an appropriate response to these profound political, economic and ecological developments. In this context the central theme of the present volume remains as valid as ever: to cope with the demands of a rapidly changing world we need an educated population, capable of taking the initiative for their own education, and motivated to continue learning throughout their lives and in many different situations. *Lifelong Learning and Higher Education* attempts to show how colleges and universities might respond to this pressing need, in particular through changes in organisational structures and teaching methods. This is the major goal of the 1991 edition of the book, just as it was for its predecessor. Naturally, we have tried to update the monograph to reflect important societal changes that have taken place in the last five years, and we have also included more recent examples of educational initiatives.

The book aims to balance theory and practice – the former because we wish to encourage academic staff to reflect more profoundly on the underlying goals of their teaching efforts, the latter because we wish to provide some useful advice on strategies for change. For this reason we have added a new final chapter to the book which provides some concrete ideas for instructors to use in their own teaching as a way of encouraging student autonomy and lifelong learning. Critical reaction to the first edition of the book was gratifyingly positive, which has encouraged us to believe that many academics share our views about the mission of higher education and our concerns about some of its shortcomings. But many readers who accepted our arguments for the importance of lifelong learning asked for help in devising ways that they might work to stimulate change in their own institutions. We hope that this revised edition will provide some help in that direction.

Acknowledgments are due to a number of organisations and individuals who contributed to the preparation of the manuscript. The research that enabled us to develop our ideas was funded in part by the Social Sciences and Research Council of Canada. Bibliographic and word-processing assistance was provided by Marlene Bechtold, Verna Keller and Susan McKenzie of the University of Waterloo. Carl Hennig gave cheerful and invaluable advice on computing problems. Lastly, our appreciation to Maryellen Weimer, of Pennsylvania State University, for her constant encouragement to prepare a second edition of the book.

Christopher Knapper and Arthur Cropley, November, 1990

Preface

The origins of this book go back several years, and reflect the authors' research interests and practical experience as teachers in higher education. We began our research collaboration over 20 years ago, and have continued working cooperatively in a variety of areas, although separated by a considerable physical distance. The present project stems from our mutual concern about the importance of university teaching and learning and how it might be improved. Arthur Cropley is Professor of Educational Psychology at the University of Hamburg, and was previously on the staff of the Unesco Institute for Education in that city. It was there that he developed many of the theoretical conceptualisations of lifelong education that are discussed in the first part of this book. Through his association with the Unesco Institute, Dr. Cropley was able to help plan and monitor implementations of lifelong education in many different parts of the world. While he has written widely on this topic, the major focus of his work has been on primary and secondary education, and it is only with the present book that the notion of lifelong education, developed by Faure and his colleagues, has been applied systematically to higher education.

Instructional methods in universities and colleges are the special interest of Christopher Knapper, who is a consultant on teaching and learning (as well as Professor of Psychology and Environmental Studies) at the University of Waterloo. A sabbatical leave in 1981–82 allowed him to work with Professor Cropley in developing ideas about how lifelong learning skills could be promoted within higher education – ideas that shaped the outline of the present book. During this leave Dr. Knapper was also fortunate enough to be able to travel widely and visit universities and colleges in many different parts of the world, ranging from Washington to Tonga. Examples from institutions he visited occur from time to time in the following pages. So too do the ideas derived from many of the hundreds of people with whom our ideas were discussed. We offer our apologies to those who may

9

recognise in print an unattributed notion developed in the course of conversation – especially in those instances where what they said has been unwittingly misrepresented.

Although examples are cited from many types of institution in contrasting parts of the world, we cannot claim to transcend the limitations of our own particular biases and experiences as students and teachers. Thus the book leans heavily upon problems and issues within the developed English-speaking nations that have long-established systems and traditions of higher education. In particular, there is a focus upon those countries with which we are most familiar, specifically Britain, Canada and the United States and to a lesser extent Australasia.

Geography is not the only limitation of the book's scope. In giving instances of educational practice – especially those that seem to consist of valuable implementations of the principles of lifelong education – we have inevitably been restricted, not only by our own knowledge, but also by constraints of space imposed by the publishers. The book attempts to introduce the concept of lifelong learning, tracing its implications for higher education, and developing a blueprint for the adoption of lifelong learning principles within colleges and universities.

Chapter 1 of the book provides a brief history of the concept of lifelong education, as developed by Faure and others, and argues the case for why lifelong learning skills are needed in contemporary society. In Chapter 2 we describe the essential characteristics of a system of lifelong education, and discuss differences between this approach and other systems with which it is often confused – such as adult or recurrent education. The third chapter focuses on the types of students who stand to benefit most from the acquisition of lifelong learning skills in higher education: what are their learning needs and how might these best be met? In Chapter 4 we turn to higher education institutions, in particular to examine how they might be transformed to reflect better the goals of lifelong education; a special concern here is with teaching methods and procedures for student assessment. Chapter 5 reviews existing approaches to teaching and learning that seem to us to have the potential for fostering lifelong learning skills in students, while Chapter 6 discusses mechanisms within post-secondary education institutions that might help transform them in directions that would place a major emphasis on the principles of lifelong education. In Chapter 7 we evaluate the teaching and learning strategies described in previous chapters in terms of the criteria spelled out at the beginning of the book, in an attempt to pinpoint most promising areas for future emphasis; we also discuss barriers to implementation of new instructional approaches, as well as ways of trying to overcome such obstacles.

The book does not advocate any single innovation, but instead draws together ideas from a wide variety of sources. As such, it describes a great deal of research. However, it is not intended primarily as a book for researchers, but for those university and college teachers – and we believe there are many – who are concerned to examine the goals of higher education, and may wish to consider alternative teaching and learning strategies that can better equip their students to become self-directed learners who can function successfully in a changing and increasingly complex world.

Christopher Knapper and Arthur Cropley, November 1983

1 Lifelong learning: an emerging approach to education

The educational 'crisis'

Although the roots of higher education can be traced back for thousands of years in many different cultures, it is surprising how many contemporary educational institutions and systems have been influenced by traditions that emanated from the great medieval European universities. Of course, distinctive patterns of higher education exist in different nations (especially in the Eastern hemisphere), but it is interesting to note the considerable similarities in the philosophy, organisation and approaches to teaching in universities throughout the world. Traditions from Britain and Germany, for example, were widely disseminated in North America. Influences from Oxford, Heidelberg and Harvard can be found in such remote locations as Fiji, Cairo, Sri Lanka and Malaysia – not surprising in view of the past political and economic dominance of Western Europe and the United States. This means that many of the central issues in modern education transcend national or regional boundaries.

Despite considerable commonality among institutions in their internal organisation and approaches to teaching and learning, the history of higher education has been marked by continual debates about the function and purpose of university education. Among the different themes are the pursuit of knowledge for its own sake versus transmission of an established body of knowledge ('research' versus 'education' or 'training'); the issue of whether universities should concentrate on preparation of a few élite professions or provide a general basic education for all citizens; the appropriateness of the university's acting as a critic of society and an agent for social change, and the question of specialist or generalist education, to cite but a few examples.

As McLoughlin (1983) has pointed out, discussion of these and similar issues has provided a topic of never ending interest to theorists,

13

politicians, employers and parents. In recent years these discussions have taken on an increasingly critical tone. For example, many modern writers argue that education today is facing a special 'crisis'. According to Coombs (1982, p. 145) this crisis which has existed since the late 1960s, has now intensified and has yielded 'critical educational challenges' that are making themselves felt not only in highly industrialised Western European and North American societies, but in virtually all nations. Such issues involve:

- *changed learning needs* (more people want to learn different things);
- *problems of financing* (reduced funding, demands for more effective use of resources);
- increased concern about *democratisation and fairness* (elimination of socioeconomic, gender and geographic inequities);
- a perceived need for *closer ties to day-to-day life* (harmonising education and culture, relating education to work, linking education to peace and preservation of the ecosystem);
- a call for *changed teaching and learning strategies* (flexible and democratic educational planning, provision of learning networks, more self-direction in learning).

Coombs supports the notion of an educational crisis by documenting the huge increases in the number of potential learners that have occurred on a worldwide basis since 1950, and which will continue up to the year 2000. He also documents 'the tightening financial squeeze' and the problem of the worsening relationship between education and employment prospects, as well as drawing attention to 'the stubborn issue of inequalities'. He calls for 'a much more comprehensive, flexible and innovative educational strategy in the coming two decades'. Such a strategy 'will require radical changes in conventional educational thinking, methods, organisations, structures and practices'. In other words, perceived shortcomings in existing education mean that a novel approach is necessary, touching upon virtually all aspects of systematic education.

Lynch (1982) has applied the idea of an educational crisis directly to higher education: he speaks of a 'legitimation crisis' (p. 8), and lists some of its dimensions. These include:

- financial stringencies and related cutbacks in higher education;
- a lack of attunement of education to the later practical training needs of individuals or to the needs of industry;

- a lack of response of post-school education to industrial and economic changes;
- failure of education to take account of rising unemployment and the educational needs which this gives rise to; and
- the need for education to offer some kind of adaptive response to social unrest and growing alienation among the young.

This crisis means that what is needed in higher education is not simply more of the same, albeit with a few minor modifications, but 'wider structural and systematic change' (p. 12). The task is thus to develop forms of education that are adapted to current economic, social and political needs of contemporary society.

Lifelong education – an alternative approach

One idea that has received considerable attention in the last 20 years is that of *lifelong* education. According to Faure (1972), this approach should be adopted as the guiding principle for reforming education at all levels and in all countries. The notion of lifelong education has since been the subject of considerable discussion, and has been spelled out in terms of its implications for schooling, teacher training, and adult education. In fact many colleges and universities already claim to promote lifelong learning through existing teaching programmes, and the terms 'lifelong learning' and 'lifelong education' have become favourite themes in institutional publicity. For example, the State University of New York has used 'the lifelong experience' as an advertising slogan for its courses – both regular and extension – and advertisements invite potential students to 'choose lifelong learning at SUNY and begin striving to meet the practical and intellectual demands of our ever more sophisticated society.'

However, lifelong learning is not always operationally defined in the same sense as that meant by Faure and his colleagues. The expression has been taken over by many institutions (or their public relations agencies) to describe familiar activities and programmes that have existed for many years (such as part time study or off-campus classes) and owe little to the recent theoretical discussions of lifelong education.

The 'meaning' of lifelong education

The uncertainty about what is meant by lifelong education is a reflection of the fact that the term is used in various ways by different writers. In the United States it has frequently been regarded as simply a new term for adult education (as in the 1976 Lifelong Learning Act, for example), and has been linked with 'alternative' educational activities such as educational brokering.* In Europe the concept has more frequently been associated with the linking of learning and work, especially through provision of paid educational leave, recurrent education, or with open learning – as exemplified by the Open University.

In a more conceptual vein, Rüegg (1974, p. 7) has referred to lifelong education as 'a utopian idea' whose main function is stimulating people to think critically about education. As Long (1974) pointed out, the idea of lifelong education can also be seen as a result of growth of 'the mystique of education'. It is thus recommended by some writers who take the view that, since education is self-evidently good, *lifelong* education must be even better! At the same time it has been criticised by Pucheu (1974, p. 375) as an 'elastic concept' which means whatever the person using the term wants it to mean.

One way of looking at lifelong education is to regard it as a rationalisation of a number of existing trends in contemporary educational theory and practice. These emerged in a variety of settings without necessarily any reference to lifelong education. They include:

- expansion of educational services outside the conventional school ages (i.e. for adults and for preschool children);
- greater interest in education as an instrument for improving the quality of life;
- concern for the development of forms of education that are more closely linked with the needs of everyday life;
- participation in decisions about education by workers, parents and members of the public;
- greater openness in goal setting; planning and administration.

Prominent among the theoretical issues that have been stressed are democratisation of education, elimination of inequality in education and achievement of higher levels of self-actualisation: these issues will be discussed separately in a later section.

---

* Educational brokering refers to the provision of advisory services for adult learners with the aim of arranging links between them and appropriate educational institutions or resources. (For example, see Heffernan, Macy, and Vickers, 1976.)

In a similar sense, lifelong education can be seen as a reaction against certain features of existing educational practice. It thus includes a rejection of authoritarianism (but not necessarily authority), unwillingness to accept that school is the dominant institution in all learning, dissatisfaction with the view that all necessary qualifications can be acquired during a brief period of learning prior to commencement of the working life, and related notions.

When viewed as a unifying principle linking existing trends and tendencies, lifelong education is a useful device for bringing together under a common heading a number of ideas and practices which, although possessing an inherent unity, would otherwise have continued to be treated as distinct from each other. The value of lifelong education as a concept is thus that it becomes possible to discern the central and definitive elements of these practices and ideas: links are seen between education and various social issues and trends that would otherwise not have been regarded as related to each other, or might not have been seen to be connected with education at all. Examples include problems arising from the increasing demand for education at a time of financial strictures, problems of obsolescence of job skills, problems of social change and issues arising from the growth in both quantity and power of the mass media. Lifelong education has the advantage of placing all of these, and many similar issues, in a single context, showing their connection with education and suggesting ways in which educational practice needs to be changed.

At least to some extent, lifelong education can also be thought of as encompassing a philosophy or model of education. In this sense, the term is used to refer to:

- a set of *goals* for education;
- a set of *procedures* for realising these goals;
- a set of *values*.

The latter specify which goals should be given precedence, which procedures are desirable and which undesirable, whose needs education should serve, what kind of society people should live in, and so on. As we shall discuss in more detail later, statements about goals, means and values are indeed to be found in the literature on lifelong education, so that regarding it as involving a 'philosophy' of education is helpful, even if many of the goals, procedures and values do not seem to arise directly out of the idea of 'lifelongness', but have been grafted on, more or less in the 'elastic' way described by Pucheu.

Lifelong education as a 'paradigm'

Perhaps the term 'philosophy' is a little pretentious here. An alternative conceptualisation is provided by Turchenko (1983) who pointed out that lifelong education is best viewed as a 'paradigm': it entails 'a system of fundamental principles which serve as a basis for raising and tackling ... problems'. What this means is that the implementation of lifelong education would not involve putting in place a special, separate system, complete in itself and intended to replace existing structures. Rather, the lifelong education paradigm provides a way of looking at what already exists in order to perceive shortcomings or see ways in which improvements could be made. One consequence of this view is that different systems of education, apparently all seeking to implement lifelong education, could easily differ markedly from each other, for instance according to national policies, educational traditions or degree of industrial development. It is also possible that markedly different educational practices could be identified as examples of the implementation of lifelong education. All would have in common, nonetheless, acceptance of the same set of fundamental principles. The first step in a discussion of the implications of lifelong education for higher education thus involves sketching out these principles. Stated as a 'paradigm' they are of necessity abstract and general: however, later sections of the book will give concrete examples of how principles can be translated into practice in a variety of settings.

The single crucial element in the notion of lifelong education is to be found in the word 'lifelong': it embraces a set of guidelines for developing educational practice ('education') in order to foster learning throughout life ('lifelong'). *Lifelong education* thus defines a set of organisational, administrative, methodological and procedural measures which accept the importance of promoting *lifelong learning*. Practical discussions in later sections of this book are concerned with how to arrange educational experiences, especially in the realm of higher education, in a way that does this effectively.

Values in lifelong education

Despite what has just been said, many proponents of lifelong education, such as Lengrand (1970) or Faure (1972), to take two early examples, argue that fostering lifelong learning would also lead to the achievement of a number of desirable educational goals that do not, in our view, arise directly out of the notion of lifelongness, but are part of any liberal-humanistic approach to education. In this sense, the ideas associated with lifelong education can be seen as a rationalisation of a number of existing trends in educational thinking which, not infrequently, came into existence without any direct reference to lifelong learning or lifelong education. Among these 'reasons' for adopting the principle of lifelong education are its potential for promoting equality of educational opportunity, its possible role in the democratisation of education, and its potential contribution to the achievement of higher levels of self-actualisation. As Cropley (1979) has pointed out, lifelong education cannot lay a unique claim to interest in promoting equality, democratisation and self-actualisation. Indeed, it is possible to imagine lifelong approaches to education which did not have these as goals, even if most people would find such forms distasteful. Thus, these 'reasons' are more accurately to be regarded as possible products of particular approaches to lifelong education, depending on the presence of an appropriate value system.

The question of values is thus of considerable importance in any discussion of lifelong education. Karpen (1980) has dealt directly with this issue, pointing out that in principle a despotic, totalitarian regime could implement lifelong education, without any intention of achieving equality or democratisation. He argues that lifelong education is therefore only to be recommended if it is offered in a framework of liberal-democratic values. According to the report of a Unesco Meeting of Experts (Unesco, 1983), lifelong education is defined as education for 'liberation', 'self-realisation' and 'self-fulfilment'. These are regarded as inevitable results of forms of education that seek to develop 'whole' beings, who possess an 'enquiring and critical mind' and are particularly capable of creativity. Lawson (1982) has gone so far as to propose that the very term 'education' automatically implies humanistic values of the kind just mentioned. Otherwise it is a matter simply of 'training', and not education at all. In this sense, then, the values that have just been discussed are not really part of the definition of lifelong education, but of education in general. Lifelong education is then seen to be essentially a policy for implementing 'education', and not a new philosophy of education. Nonetheless it would be fair to say that values of this kind have become so strongly associated with writings on lifelong education that they now form part of its definition, although they are not inherent in the notion of 'lifelong', and not exclusively associated with lifelong education.

Indeed, as will be seen in later discussions, lifelong education may truly be a policy that offers special opportunities to achieve equality and self-actualisation. For instance, the idea that personal development occurs throughout the entire life span, a point of view that has found increasing acceptance in psychological thinking (e.g. Horn, 1982), coupled with the notion that education is capable of making a contribution to this personal development, implies that lifelong education would be uniquely placed to facilitate lifelong self-actualisation. In a similar vein, it can also be argued that extending systematic state-subsidised learning opportunities beyond the age of anywhere between 12 and 30, according to the society in question, would promote the achievement of true educational equality, since this would enhance the possibility for learners to equal or exceed the achievements of those who had had better opportunities in early life. These possible outcomes of lifelong education may be mentioned as reasons for adopting the concept, despite the risk of teleological thinking that this entails.

Lifelong learning

Lifelong education can be thought of as a set of organisational and procedural guidelines for educational practice aimed at fostering learning throughout life. It is important to make clear at once that what is meant here by 'learning' is not the spontaneous, day-to-day learning of everyday life, such as when people learn to proffer the correct amount in payment after bus fares are increased. It is perfectly clear that such learning is lifelong, no doubt always has been, and will continue to be, regardless of the pronouncements of educational theorists. The kind of lifelong learning that is the object of lifelong education is what Tough (1971) called 'deliberate' learning. Such learning has the following definitive characteristics:

- It is intentional – learners are aware that they are learning;
- It has a definite, specific goal and it is not aimed at vague generalisations such as 'developing the mind';
- This goal is the reason why the learning is undertaken (i.e. it is not motivated simply by factors like boredom);
- The learner intends to retain what has been learned for a considerable period of time.

This distinction between deliberate learning and spontaneous, unplanned, even unconscious learning is important in the present context because it permits a differentiation between the lifelong learning that is a normal and natural part of everyday life and the systematic, purposeful, organised learning that lifelong education procedures seek to foster. Of course the distinction is to some extent artificial, since the same psychological processes are involved. Organised learning – such as that which takes place during a university class – obviously interacts with day-to-day learning, for instance in the sense that learning in the classroom can be facilitated or inhibited by learning in everyday life, and vice versa. Nonetheless, a distinction, albeit an artificial one, is essential for the purposes of the present book. The whole question of the interrelationship of deliberate learning and day-to-day learning, and of the significance of this interaction for higher education, will be discussed in more detail in a later section.

The basic idea that not only day-to-day learning but also deliberate learning can and should occur throughout each person's lifetime is by no means new. It is to be found in ancient writings (see Asian Institute, 1970), and was emphasised in the works of earlier European educational theorists such as Comenius and Matthew Arnold. The term 'lifelong education' appeared in English language writings almost 70 years ago (Richmond, 1973) and many of the main contemporary ideas about lifelong education had already been stated immediately after the Second World War (e.g. Jacks, 1946). Nonetheless, as we have already mentioned, the past two decades have been marked by considerable discussion of the importance of lifelong learning, and descriptions of the personnel, processes, methods and materials, institutions and administrative and organisational conditions necessary for its facilitation. In this respect, then, recent interest in lifelong education can be regarded as a new phenomenon (Hummel, 1977).

The need for lifelong learning

Change. The reasons that have led to this increased interest in the promotion of lifelong learning, and that give it an urgency and relevance that was lacking in earlier times, are social, economic and cultural in nature (de Sanctis, 1977). They arise from the phenomenon of change that is a major element in contemporary life (Cropley, 1977). McClusky (1974, p. 101) made the connection between change and lifelong learning in a particularly succinct way, pointing out that 'continuous change requires continuous learning'. Agoston (1975) referred to a 'scientific-technological revolution', while Stonier (1979) mentioned the 'two revolutions' of ordinary life: technological change and changes in the information domain.

Obviously, change is not necessarily a bad thing in itself: there may well be aspects of life and areas of the globe where more rapid change is desirable. However, the present cycle of change has two features that distinguish it from the process of development which has been an inevitable accompaniment of the evolution of human culture. Both are potentially destructive. The first is the rapidity with which changes are occurring: in the past they have always been slow relative to the life expectancy of a single human being, so that people could adapt themselves to a set of conditions which remained more or less constant during their lifetimes (Knowles, 1975). The present set of changes, by contrast, is occurring so rapidly that the cycle may repeat itself several times within a single lifetime. The second feature of change in the modern world is that it is global: it transcends regional and national boundaries. The crucial point for the present discussion is that people must be able to adjust to change that is at once both rapid and sweeping. Earlier models of education, in which most deliberate learning is supposed to occur in childhood and youth, and most learning in the adult years is expected to be of the everyday kind, are no longer appropriate, since they are based on the idea that adulthood is simply a time for reapplying old learning.

Change in work. The most obvious area in which rapid change occurs involves the world of work: factors such as technological progress, development of manufacturing techniques, emergence of new products and increases in knowledge are combining to produce a situation in which some jobs are simply ceasing to exist, while in others the basic skills are changing so extensively and rapidly that it is no longer possible to acquire them once and for all during an initial education and then spend the rest of one's life applying them. This is true not only of manual skills and trades, but also of the professions. The whole printing industry, for instance, is in the process of being transformed by the disappearance of traditional typesetting methods and their replacement by word processing procedures. To take another example, diagnostic procedures in medicine are rapidly being transformed by technological advances, while chemotherapy is constantly altered by new discoveries. Dubin (1974) has shown that the 'half life' of an average engineering class taught in an American university (the period of time during which half of its content becomes obsolete) is diminishing continually, so that what is being learned today may be irrelevant in only a few years. Changes of this kind mean that it may well be necessary, even for workers at fairly humble levels, to renew, upgrade or even change basic job qualifications at least once during a normal lifetime.

Social change. The effects of the scientific-technological revolution are not, however, confined to the world of work. The increasing availability of information through the media means, among other things, that children are exposed, to a hitherto unknown extent, to many socialising agencies lying outside the family. Not infrequently people and situations depicted in the media (particularly television) may compete with parents, offering conflicting or contradictory sets of standards or values. One result is a decrease in the importance of the family as an educational agency. This is further affected by factors such as social dislocation resulting from rapid urbanisation, the greatly increased leisure seen in some societies, unemployment or changes in the role of work and relationships between workers and supervisors, and rapidly changing sex roles. Even these problems seem trivial compared to the immense social, economic and political changes occurring in Eastern Europe at the end of the 1980s which will continue to have an important impact on people's lifestyles and value systems for years to come. The effects of sociocultural change are potentially disastrous, since they bring with them the possibility of a 'collapse of values' (Aujaleu, 1973, p. 25). If people are unable to develop new kinds of relationships with other people and accept altered social roles, changes of the kind just outlined constitute a threat to psychological well-being (Suchodolski, 1976). Change thus brings psychological dangers and difficulties in situations where people are unable to cope with it. Lifelong learning is seen as a constructive response that can help to avert these dangers: it is regarded as a device for helping people find patterns of life that satisfy their social, emotional and aesthetic needs, even in a rapidly evolving society.

Special groups. Lifelong education is regarded by many writers as a concept that is particularly promising for meeting the newly recognised educational needs of special groups in society who are placed at an educational disadvantage by traditional education. These groups include people of low socio-economic status, migrant or transient workers, the handicapped, rural people and women. In general, these are groups who either found it difficult to learn effectively in schools during childhood (for instance because of lack of insight into the usefulness of school learning, or lack of familiarity with the language of instruction), who were barred from attending by physical factors such as distance, or who were prematurely forced out of the educational system before exhausting its possibilities, (for instance by the need to go to work and help support a family or by a value system that dictated they did not 'need' any further education). Indeed, it is clearly arguable that a system in which even school level learning tasks could be undertaken at many ages would offer special prospects for members of these and similar groups.

Division of labour. Gelpi (1980) has taken this approach a step further by drawing attention to the interaction between the system of education and the system of production. Education, he argues, serves to equip certain people with knowledge, skills, attitudes, even a self-image, appropriate to the fulfilling of particular functions in a society's work hierarchy. It is thus, in a sense, an instrument for assigning roles, status and power to individuals and groups. One result of this is that lifelong education could increase the gaps between those high in the pecking order and those occupying lower positions: in other words it could increase the social division of labour. Nonetheless, appropriate forms of lifelong education could, by disseminating knowledge (in the broadest sense of the term) among workers, give them more power to make management decisions in areas which closely affect their lives. Hence lifelong education has the potential to function as an emancipatory force in society.

Demographic change. A further aspect of the crisis referred to earlier derives from demographic changes which have been evident for a considerable time and are now approaching the acute phase: populations in Western European and North American societies are becoming older. At a recent conference in Hamburg, for instance, it was pointed out that by the year 2000 one third of the population of that city state will be 60 years of age or over. In the United States, by the year 2030 the age 'pyramid' will instead be a rectangle, with about 6 per cent of the population in each five-year age cohort. About 15 per cent of all US college students are already aged 35 or over. The other side of the coin is that there are fewer people in the age group at which people traditionally enter higher education.

For the universities this raises the question of how they are to justify their existence and expand their clientele at a time of budgetary constraints *and* when many politicians and members of the public are calling for increased access to higher education. One solution is to try and attract more 'non-traditional' students, for example older students and those within the conventional age group who have no tradition of university study by virtue of socioeconomic status, race or ethnic group status, or sex. This has indeed happened in some countries, such as Canada and the USA, where extensive opportunities for part-time study have allowed greater participation of older students who have family and work responsibilities. In other systems (e.g. Britain), however, the proportion of part time students has scarcely altered since 1981 (McIlroy, 1987), and the number of older students has grown only slightly.

Apart from the need to find new students as sources of revenue, universities have an important role in helping societies cope with the effects of demographic change. It has already become apparent that there is no longer an inexhaustible supply of youngsters to enter the work world as beginners. In the Federal Republic of Germany during 1990, for instance, many apprenticeships could not be filled due to a scarcity of school leavers. One result in some countries has been the opening up of apprenticeships to 30 and 40-year-olds. To cite a related example, some police forces in the United Kingdom have begun accepting recruits in their forties. There is an urgent need for universities to play their part in training adults to undertake tasks that have traditionally been the domain of the young. Recent political events in the countries of Eastern Europe have added a new dimension to this task. Massive retraining programmes will become necessary for people who have already been in the work force for many years. To take one example, thousands of school principals have lost their jobs in the eastern part of Germany, and successors for their positions must be found and trained quickly. Business managers, scientists and econo-mists, not to mention technicians and engineers, must be retrained at university level in Hungary, Poland and Czechoslovakia. It seems unlikely that the universities of these countries will be equal to the task they face unless they are able to adopt quite novel approaches.

An adequate response to the changed circumstances just outlined requires more than simply better advertising or more aggressive recruitment of students. This view is supported by findings on participation of adults in existing educational opportunities. In the

United States, for instance, the average adult spends some 500 hours a year engaging in 'learning projects' (Tough, 1971), and in Europe – to take the example of Norway (Eide, 1980) – well over half of all systematic learning takes place outside schools at all levels. Yet only about 20 per cent of adult learning occurs within the framework of organised adult education, and only a small proportion of adults ever participate in such activities (Eccleston and Schmidt, 1979; Stock, 1979). Furthermore, both in the USA and Western Europe, the best predictor of participation in higher education outside the traditional ages is level of previous education. Essentially, only the 'educational junkies' are being reached at present, while at least half the population can be classified as non-participants. Thus promoting broader participation in college and university study will require more than mere administrative changes, since adults, despite being perfectly capable of learning, do not make use of the opportunities already available. A summary of some aspects of this problem is to be found in Cropley (1988).

Recapitulation

It is increasingly being argued that educational systems in both highly and less developed countries are faced with a crisis that demands radical rethinking of how education is to be delivered. In particular, lifelong learning is seen as the key, and forms of education are required that are capable of fostering such learning. These forms, referred to in this book as defining a system of 'lifelong education', involve not only administrative and organisational elements of education, but also instructional content and materials, teaching and learning strategies, and evaluation. The balance of this book will be concerned with outlining what the promotion of lifelong learning implies in these areas, and with showing what this means for the practice of higher education.

Inevitably, a major thrust of the book involves the provision of appropriate educational experiences for adults. However, we are not only concerned here with novel programmes for new client groups, but also with the implications of lifelong education for relatively conventional institutions of higher education. In this sense the present volume differs sharply from many other discussions of the practical consequences of lifelong learning for higher education. Higher education merits special study because of its particular importance in helping to develop and implement a system of lifelong education. This importance derives from the prestige and influence exercised by universities and colleges within the educational systems of most countries. More particularly, institutions of higher education play a major role in the training of teachers, where they provide not only theoretical principles (such as a belief in the importance of lifelong learning), but also practical experiences and examples – for instance, teaching strategies that are themselves orientated to learning throughout life. In this way it seems plausible that the models and precepts set by higher education will have ramifications for the practice of teaching and learning at all levels. Hence higher education is what Williams (1977, p. 17) calls the 'dominant force' that sets the tone. It is frequently in universities and colleges that educational changes are initially elaborated, before filtering down to the school or out into the domain of informal and non-formal education.

2   Lifelong education as a system

Systems for supporting learning

Learning is a normal and natural process that occurs at all ages and in all kinds of settings (see for example Stephens, 1967). It does not depend upon contact with teachers or even other people, although it will be seen later that such individuals often play an important role in fostering learning. It can occur in the absence of organisational conditions deliberately planned to promote it, and does not require awareness on the part of learners that they are learning. Nonetheless, neither the presence of an organised learning system nor awareness that learning is taking place necessarily impedes it - such factors may even help. The acceptance of the need for highly organised, institutionalised support for learning is, in fact, so widely accepted that virtually all countries make provision for systematic education.

Education as schooling

There was a time when the young learned work and life skills by watching adults performing them, and when it would have been incomprehensible to have talked about education in any other terms. Learners served masters of a craft or trade, watched them at work, helped with manual tasks, participated in the simpler aspects of the job, practised the necessary skills and in this way slowly acquired appropriate knowledge and techniques, as well as associated attitudes, values and self-image. Learning in this way has by no means ceased to exist. Indeed, it is still very important, particularly in less developed nations. Nonetheless, with the rise of technology the kind of 'non-formal learning' (Coombs and Ahmed, 1974) just described became less and less efficient. As a result, the idea has gained strength that education is something that precedes real life, should provide the young in advance with the skills they will need in the future, and requires a

28

specialised learning environment watched over by experts. The child has come to be seen as a receptacle that has to be filled with knowledge via a set of stages and forms that together define a system of formal education, usually centred on schools. The latter are regarded as essential for learning, and indeed many parents place high value on their children's attending a 'good school' – a term that usually implies they are dominated by the 'high' culture of the society in question.

Thus not only has education come to be equated with schools, but schooling has come to be seen as something that precedes real life, or even constitutes a kind of qualification or precondition for entering adulthood. The function of schooling is regarded as communicating to the young knowledge and skills that will prove valuable in the adult life to come, even if they are of minimal relevance to immediate, day-to-day experiences. Because of their role in preparing students for citizenship, schools have also come to be regarded as primarily concerned with the transmission of useful information and skills that can eventually be applied more or less directly in life. In other words, schooling is seen as a way of collecting ready-made answers, rather than of developing general tactics for acquiring information, coping with new situations or planning and evaluating learning activities.

Consequences for formal education

This state of affairs has had a number of consequences for systems of education. It means that, until recently, relatively little attention has been paid to learning processes and learning needs in adults, despite the fact that these are the very people who have to cope in their day-to-day lives with the change phenomena which have already been mentioned. Although adult education already exists, and even involves considerable segments of the population in some societies, it is still largely viewed as a supplement to 'real' education offered in schools. The relationship of lifelong education to adult education will be discussed more fully in a later section.

In passing it might be noted that a second neglected group consists of children who have not yet reached the conventional school age. Once again, there has been a tendency to regard these youngsters as either learning in much the same way as school age children do, or else as incompetent or incapable of rational or logical thinking. This approach is inconsistent with research findings which emphasise that even very young children are 'competent' (see Stone, Murphy and Smith, 1972), or which give great weight to the importance of early childhood as a crucial stage of development in intellectual, social and personal development.

The view that education and schooling are identical leads to some further problems. For example, learning may come to be seen by students as something that has little connection with their lives (although it may prove to be useful in the future), and thus learners may become 'passive'. What is meant by this term is that students come to expect that learning experiences will be planned and supervised by other people, and decisions about results of learning will be made by outsiders. These consequences are mentioned here because they are seen as partly a result of the organisational structure of conventional education. They will be dealt with in greater detail in the following chapter, which focuses on learners and learning processes.

A system of lifelong education

As we have already mentioned, lifelong education may be regarded as being, to a certain extent, a reaction against the traditional model that has just been outlined, or as an approach to organising education that could avoid some of these problems. Put somewhat differently, one major characteristic of lifelong education as an organising principle for the provision of educational services is its rejection of the view that organised, systematic support of learning should be confined to childhood. A second characteristic is its rejection of the idea that worthwhile, purposeful learning occurs only in special settings set aside specifically for such purposes. Hubermann (1979) has pointed out that justifying lifelong education by criticising existing institutions has become almost a cliché, since this approach is to be found in almost all discussions of the topic. Nonetheless, a brief reexamination of the typical criticisms of existing formal education is necessary for the purposes of this book, since it has such important consequences for higher education. The relevant discussion is to be found not only in the present section, but also in both earlier and later ones.

'Concept characteristics'

In addition to the two criteria mentioned above, lifelong education as an organising principle has a number of characteristics that derive not so much from a criticism of traditional practice as from the various goals and values spelled out in Chapter 1. Dave (1973) developed a list of 'concept characteristics' which have been restated by Cropley (1980) as a set of definitive principles for a system of lifelong education. In such a system, education would:

- last the whole life of each individual;
- lead to the systematic acquisition, renewal, and upgrading of knowledge, skills and attitudes, as this became necessary in response to the constantly changing conditions of modern life, with the ultimate goal of promoting self-fulfilment of each individual;
- be dependent on people's increasing ability and motivation to engage in self-directed learning activities;
- acknowledge the contribution of all available educational influences, including formal, non-formal and informal.

The characteristics above define an educational system that would start prior to the normal school age, and would continue beyond the end of formal schooling. It would encompass many learning settings including the home, the community, the place of work, clubs and societies and would involve many different learning and teaching strategies. The present book assumes that traditional institutions such as schools, universities and colleges would continue to have an important role, although in their present form they encompass only a narrow range of learning settings and approaches. Proponents of lifelong education emphasise, among other things, two important principles that are of relevance here. On the one hand, traditional educational institutions do not enjoy a monopoly on educating people; on the other, it is highly undesirable that they continue to function in a kind of splendid isolation from other learning settings.

Differences from adult education

It is quite obvious that a system of lifelong education would deal predominantly with adult clients, if for no other reason than that in the normal course of events most people spend far more of their lives as adults than as children or young people. In other words, the principle of lifelong education has important consequences for adult education. This does not, however, mean that the term 'lifelong education' is simply another way of saying 'adult education'. While proponents of

31

lifelong education obviously have much to learn from people already working in the field of adult education, the reverse is also true.

Discussions at a European conference on adult education held a few years ago made it plain that the overwhelming majority of the practitioners in attendance found it difficult to accept that learning in the post-school years is as important as that during the conventional school ages. For instance, they dismissed as absurd the idea that, in principle, *all* adults should be regarded as the natural and normal clients of adult education, pointing out, among other things, that this would be simply too expensive. A major problem was that these professionals implicitly saw adult education as a fringe or 'frill' activity in which only small amounts of public money could be invested. Furthermore, they accepted a model of teaching and learning processes based heavily on traditional schools, and regarded any expansion of adult education as implying larger numbers of people engaging in traditional activities. As we have already stated, however, and shall discuss in more detail in Chapter 3, a system of lifelong education could not consist of a mere extension of school-like activities throughout each person's lifetime. Putting this bluntly, although there is an overlap between the ideas encompassed by the notions of lifelong education and adult education, in the sense that both are concerned with the provision of learning experiences to adults, the similarities go little further.

Although adult educators may pay lip service to the importance of breaking away from the traditional school model, in fact most of them still see themselves on the fringe of the conventional system, playing the role of handmaidens or poor cousins. In many cases they would be the first to shy away from the consequences of truly accepting the notion that it is just as important for adults to engage in systematic learning as for children. For instance, the point of view that schools are largely there to prepare children for participation in learning as adults would be regarded with suspicion by many practising adult educators. They would also question the assertion that to say, 'We can't possibly afford to provide adult education for more than half of adults' is as reprehensible as to accept that 'We can't afford to provide schooling for more than half of all children'. While our line of argument here perhaps represents an extreme position, it is certainly true that a full-fledged acceptance of the promotion of lifelong learning as the guiding principle for educational systems would involve a very strong shift in thinking in the direction spelled out above.

In summary, then, despite the emphasis here on the importance of learning in adulthood, lifelong education goes far beyond conventional adult education. It envisages a drastic change in the relationship of school level learning and post-school learning, in the purpose and status of systematic learning at various ages, in the worth of different kinds of learning and in the methods and procedures to be used at different age levels. Adoption of lifelong education would greatly enhance the importance of adult education. But it would also require adult educators to make considerable changes in their roles, responsibilities, relationships with other post-school agencies, teaching and learning methods and evaluation procedures.

Before leaving this subject, we should recognise that a variety of terms are used in the educational literature, and by practitioners, to refer to a wide range of learning experiences available to adults. In the present section we have talked of 'adult education'. Other expressions include continuing education, extramural studies, extension teaching, recurrent education, further education, to name the most familiar. No attempt is made here to distinguish these different terms. More important for the present purpose is to point out that some aspects of all these educational approaches are consistent with the principles of lifelong learning (e.g. study tours, factory-based courses, joint programmes with local museums and libraries), while other aspects are less so (e.g. a traditional lecture course offered in the evening). Use of an educational slogan is no guarantee of a matching educational philosophy.

Rejection of lifelong schooling

A possible misunderstanding needs to be dealt with at this point. This is the notion that a system of lifelong education would extend the values and methods of traditional institutions to all aspects of each person's entire lifetime. If lifelong education were to mean, in effect, lifelong schooling, it would become the 'trap' about which Illich and Verne (1975) warned, condemning people, to use Dauber and Verne's (1976) metaphor, to school 'for the term of their natural life'. Lifelong education as a set of principles for organising systematic provision of learning opportunities is thus not a form of 'educational imperialism' (Karpen, 1980) but an alternative approach to the provision of learning experiences. In the balance of the present chapter more will be said about what this means for the educational system, while its implications for educational institutions will be spelled out in Chapter 4. In Chapter

3, the consequences of lifelong education for learners and learning will be discussed in greater detail.

Vertical integration

The first and the most obvious organisational principle of lifelong education is that it must facilitate learning throughout the entire life span. What this means is that the temporally separate elements of the education system, such as preschool, elementary schooling, secondary schooling, initial post-school education and further education, would all be coordinated with each other in such a way that each of the separate stages or levels would function both as a continuation of the previous stage and a preparation for the next. This linking up of different temporal stages or phases is referred to as *vertical integration*.

It might well be argued that these types of links already exist, especially as it is usually necessary to obtain some kind of lower qualification before proceeding to a higher stage. However, what is meant here by 'coordination' is considerably more than regulation of the speed and direction of movement through the system. For instance, it would be necessary for the system to be organised in such a way that a particular learner could move forward or backward. It should also be possible for different people to enter the same level of the system (for instance tertiary education) at different ages. Vertical integration would require that movement within the system be based not only on a decision about whether the necessary basic knowledge had been mastered, but also on whether learners had developed appropriate attitudes towards learning skills to enable them to continue to learn after formal education has ceased, and an understanding of the relationship between learning at differing age levels, etc.

Horizontal integration

We have already pointed out that lifelong education would not mean lifelong schooling. For one thing, it would be absurd to imagine adults continually returning to school throughout their lives. The prospect of being subjected to lifelong control by conventional teachers is also an unpleasant one that many people would reject out of hand. Thus, especially in the case of learning occurring beyond the conventional school ages, it is apparent that the majority of learning experiences will take place outside the present formal system of education. Indeed, there is evidence that this is what happens at present to a large extent. For example, Eide (1980) reported that in Norway in the early 1970s only 40 per cent of all learning was carried on under the auspices of the formal educational system, and he estimated that the proportion was falling. The remaining learning, although systematic and purposeful in the sense of the Tough definition already referred to, went on at work, in the family, in the course of leisure activities and so on. Cropley (1981) has discussed in greater detail the educative role of the workplace, zoos, museums, libraries, clubs, churches, political parties and similar organisations. Even recreational activities such as playing sport, going to the cinema, perhaps even drinking with friends in a pub can be seen as having a significant educational value. One element in systematic lifelong education would be acknowledgement of the worth of learning in such settings, strengthening of it and even incorporation of some of its major features into learning within institutions. The coupling of learning in traditional institutions to learning in settings such as those just mentioned constitutes 'horizontal integration'.

An interesting discussion emphasising the need to link learning with real life has recently been offered by Brown, Collins and Duguid (1989), although they do not use the term lifelong learning in their paper. The authors distinguish between 'decontextualised' and 'situated' learning. The former occurs in formal educational institutions and rests on an assumption that knowledge is a separate entity existing independently of the contexts in which it is applied. In contrast, situated learning occurs in everyday settings and is one of the normal products of life. Brown et al. give the example of learning a native language, where it is estimated that children acquire new words at a rate of 5,000 per year from the age of about 12 months in the course of their daily lives, and are able to use these words both appropriately and correctly. On the other hand, in the classroom students are able to learn no more than 100–200 words per year, and this vocabulary is often used incorrectly, since it is acquired by means of abstract definitions and frequently learned out of context. Much the same can be said of other content areas, with the result that children can pass exams in a discipline, but may be unable to apply such knowledge in real–world situations.

The authors go on to argue that learning should occur via participation in 'authentic' activities, which they define as 'the ordinary practices of the culture'. At present, someone who wishes to learn a new skill has two alternative, more or less competing, options. The first involves carrying out the activity in question in a real-life setting with the help of someone who knows how to do it (e.g. by means of an apprenticeship). The second is to learn it in an 'academic' way by going to school. Unfortunately, however, the way in which, for instance, mathematics is taught in school often bears little resemblance to what practitioners of mathematics actually do. And the same is true for other skills. Brown *et al.* suggest that the concept of apprenticeship should be extended to areas such as language, mathematics, and history. Students would learn better by means of participation in authentic activity in normal situations – which should include the social and cultural interactions that are part of such settings. The authors call this learning/ teaching approach 'cognitive apprenticeship', and give examples from the teaching of mathematics of how this kind of learning could be promoted. In one example, students bring examples of mathematical problems encountered in real life to school, and attempt to find solutions with the help of the teacher and other class members. In another, students make up stories in which mathematical principles are demonstrated in action – for instance, multiplication of 12 by 4 is learned by means of a story involving 12 jars each with 4 butterflies in it. The authors argue it is possible, by means of learning through cognitive apprenticeship, to go beyond the level of simple practical examples and achieve a level of abstraction, generalisation, and articulation (in the sense of communication) comparable to what is possible by means of decontextualised learning, while at the same time acquiring the additional context knowledge associated with situated learning.

To return to the theme of educational imperialism, it is important to emphasise once again that lifelong education would not mean the imposing of values of the formal educational system on all elements of life, despite the importance of recognising the worth of learning in non-school settings. In order to facilitate discussion of this point, it is useful to think in terms of two kinds of educational influences to which people are exposed. The first consists of institutionalised influences such as the school and similar agencies, while the second comprises non-institutionalised educational influences of which a number of examples have just been given. Although, in principle, learning in all settings would be of interest in the context of lifelong education, there must be areas of experience that remain strictly private. A small child playing with a grandparent might well be learning, but it would somehow be repugnant to try and systematise this process.

Indeed, Walker (1980) has made the point that achievement of systematic horizontal integration runs the risk of trying to organise the unorganisable. It seems arrogant or repulsive for organised education to turn its attention to these newly discovered learning arenas. Thus the achievement of horizontal integration, in which learning in all settings is seen to be interrelated, must tread a narrow path between educational imperialism and worthwhile reform. One guiding principle that may help to achieve horizontal integration while avoiding imperialism involves ensuring that the flow of influence between educational domains is reasonably balanced. In other words, the influence of the non-formal domain on events in the formal system should be at least as strong as the influence in the other direction.

A broader definition of education

The two principles that have just been outlined, especially when taken in combination with learning principles to be discussed in detail in Chapter 3, lead to an altered notion of what is meant by 'education'. Instead of being regarded as fixed or static, 'an asset to be received' or 'a legacy to be acquired' during childhood and youth, as is presently the case (see Pineau, 1980), education would take place at all ages and in many different settings. The implementation of vertical and horizontal integration would have implications for all aspects of an educational system, including its goals and content, the institutions upon which it is based, the structure of responsibility and authority, forms and methods of financing, its legislative basis, as well as the nature of credentials and the procedures through which they are acquired.

To take one example, the relationship between different learning settings such as factories, programmes offered by professional associations, colleges, and universities would alter in such a way that boundaries between them would become 'porous' – learners would be able to transfer backwards and forwards between settings, or select various mixtures of settings. The idea of the 'normal' age of entry into a particular institution would be radically altered, as would the notion of the 'drop-out', since different people would leave and enter various educational settings at different times during their lives, or would remain in particular settings for differing periods of time. Many settings not normally regarded as having a substantial educational role, such as museums or zoos, libraries, radio stations, churches, committee rooms and so on, would have their contribution to purposeful learning acknowledged and emphasised. These changes would not simply be quantitative in nature, but would also be qualitative. In other words, it is not simply a matter of increasing the number of settings that are regarded as important in post-school education, but of changing the nature of the relationships among them and of the things that go on within them.

The notion that learning in institutions within the framework of lifelong education would need to be closely linked with educational experiences in life itself is more than simply a clang association with the word 'life' that occurs in the expression 'lifelong education'. Education is always related to the society in which it occurs. An education that continued throughout each person's lifetime would, however, need to be particularly closely linked with fundamental social, economic, even political issues in the society concerned. Otherwise, it would move in the direction of lifelong schooling, a conceptualisation that we have already specifically rejected. One of the major justifications of a system of lifelong education, discussed in Chapter 1, is the phenomenon of change in everyday life. Thus, lifelong education would be closely bound to the transformations taking place in day-to-day life. This link would include not only scientific and technical aspects of a society, but also cultural, economic and even religious elements.

Liberal education and the core curriculum

In the field of higher education, what might be thought of as an early blueprint for lifelong education was provided by Cardinal Newman, who articulated the principles of 'liberal' education (Newman, 1973:1852). Newman's writing had a marked influence on post-secondary education, especially in the United States, and provided a philosophical basis for many college curricula and degree programmes in the 'liberal arts'. Like Faure, Newman was concerned with the type of person moulded by experience with formal education. Ideally, for Newman, this would be a type of 'renaissance man' (in Newman's day the notion of a renaissance woman had less currency) who could use the knowledge, skills and attitudes learned in university to guide him through the rest of life.

In its North American manifestation the planning of a liberal arts programme primarily involved decisions about curriculum. Many institutions adopted the notion of a 'core' of courses that would supposedly provide students with an introduction to basic areas of knowledge and inquiry. A typical liberal arts core curriculum, for example, might include a course in English, a foreign language, a laboratory science, plus mathematics or perhaps symbolic logic or the history of science. (Other approaches include the University of Chicago's 'great books' syllabus and Keele University's foundation year.) During the 1970s, the North American liberal arts curriculum lost some ground to specialised, professionally-oriented programmes. However, the idea of a common core of courses is far from dead, and indeed in the past decade two prominent North American universities – Harvard and Toronto – reintroduced the idea for students in the arts and humanities, and triggered a lively debate within the higher education literature (see Keller, 1982).

Professional and vocational education

Although the term 'liberal education' has a somewhat grandiose ring to it, and is one that is often contrasted with professional, technical, or vocational education, Newman was quite clear that universities should prepare their graduates for working life. This is hardly surprising since the early students at Oxford and Cambridge were in a sense preparing for jobs in the church, in teaching, at the court and within the legal system. Harvard too was established in the seventeenth century to prepare men for the professions (medicine, law, etc). The issue of course is not whether universities should prepare their students for life and work, but rather what form that preparation should take – a general education, as in the liberal arts curriculum, or more specialised training, as found in the professional schools.

Universities have never forsaken vocational education, but it is interesting to note that many nations have established alternative institutions with a specific mandate to serve vocational training needs that the universities, presumably, were not meeting satisfactorily. Thus, for example, the Grandes Écoles in France and the German Technische Hochschulen were established to provide a cadre of highly trained professionals and technicians. More recently the British polytechnics, set up for the most part during the mid-1960s, were created with similar aims in mind and in the hope that they would provide a much needed stimulus to industrial revival.

Despite the special provisions made for educating professionals, both in technical institutions and traditional universities, there is by no means universal agreement about what constitutes appropriate professional education – either in terms of aims, content areas, or – especially – instructional methods. In many instances the members of the profession itself – through their licensing associations – have had a major, if indirect, say in university curricula leading to professional qualification. However, even where such professional associations are strong, the profession prestigious and of long standing, there can be disagreements about appropriate training, often producing new initiatives in educational programmes and teaching methods. A notable example (which we discuss further in Chapter 6) is the field of medicine, where certain universities have developed radical alternatives to the traditional curriculum and have introduced novel approaches to learning that are, we shall argue, highly consistent with our criteria for lifelong education.

Recapitulation

The implementation of lifelong education would have sweeping implications for schools and universities. Elements of the total social system, for example, would receive reinforced attention because of their obvious connection with the educational system, and many familiar roles and institutions would be seen in a new light. For example, the workplace would be seen as one of the major learning subsystems of society, one in which a great deal is already learned and even more could be learned if its learning potential were adequately acknowledged and emphasised. However, it is also apparent that cooperation among the different elements of an educational system, as the idea of 'system' has been defined in this chapter, could not be based purely upon conventional teaching and learning strategies. In other words, the educational system discussed here could not be based on traditional school learning. This means that implementation of lifelong education would have implications for teachers, for learners and for learning activities. This is the theme of Chapter 3.

3 Learners and learning processes

The meaning of 'learning'

The importance of distinguishing between everyday learning and deliberate learning has already been mentioned in Chapter 1. Nonetheless, this distinction is sufficiently important to warrant more detailed discussion: as Lawson (1982) pointed out, without a 'tighter' definition of learning the whole notion of lifelong learning would become trivial. He distinguishes (p. 103) between simple exposure to the 'general mass of formative influences', with consequent 'general learning which any intelligent being undergoes in adapting to circumstances', and 'planned, intentional preparation', which is not simply a reaction to day-to-day happenings but 'a way of short-circuiting personal experience by drawing upon the accumulated experience of others'. It is the second kind of learning that is the object of systematic lifelong education, not the first. It should be mentioned in passing, however, that learning in ordinary life settings is by no means ignored: the principle of horizontal integration places great emphasis on such learning, partly because it is important in its own right, and partly because of the possibility for improving systematised learning by linking it with everyday learning, or even by incorporating some informal processes into formal settings.

Institutionalised and non-institutionalised learning

Cropley (1980) has provided a schematic conceptualisation of educational development in Figure 3.1. Non-institutionalised influences act in conjunction with systematic, planned education to mould a given individual, who is thus the product of both kinds of influence.

Influences in the area designated 'A' take effect with or without conscious awareness on the part of learners and 'teachers'. Even when

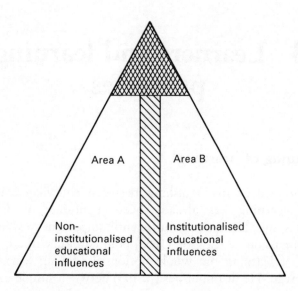

Figure 3.1 *Educational influences on the individual*

such factors are to some extent conscious and deliberate, they are not formalised or institutionalised. Area B consists of activities deliberately planned for promoting learning. Lifelong education stresses that Area B should become more open to the influence of Area A – in other words, formal or institutionalised learning settings and procedures should:

- be recognised as comprising only a portion of the total spectrum of educational influences;
- acknowledge the importance of learning occurring outside the formal education system;
- be more open to interaction with everyday learning influences.

The learning continuum

Strictly speaking, these different kinds of influence comprise not two separate domains as Figure 3.1 may seem to imply, but a continuum. This ranges from the most unorganised and uninstitutionalised kinds of learning activity, which take place in the course of day-to-day life, to the most highly organised kinds characteristic of formal education. Figure 3.2 provides a diagrammatic representation of this continuum. The settings listed along the horizontal axis are merely examples of kinds of learning having different degrees of systematisation, not definite labels for the regions in question, while relative distances between examples have no significance. All learners engage in activities from different parts of the spectrum, although the proportion of time spent on activities of a particular kind may differ markedly from person to person.

Generally, it is recognised (e.g. Karpen, 1980) that not all learning settings can be subjected to organisation and systematisation – some aspects of life are sacrosanct. This means that there is a barrier separating those learning settings that organisation could in principle 'improve' from those that must always remain private and personal, although the position of this barrier might well be dependent upon the values of a particular society. The placing of the barrier could be seen as defining the degree of educational imperialism. For instance, in some societies television is regarded primarily as an educational tool, while in others it is used almost exclusively as a means of entertainment. The implementation of lifelong education would simply mean increased recognition of activities at the left-hand side of Figure 3.2. However, it is important to repeat that this shifting of the barrier would not mean making the less organised experiences more like school, but could just

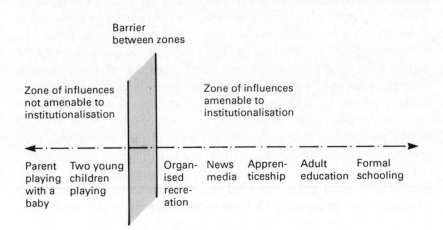

Figure 3.2 *The continuum of influences on learning*

as easily mean making school experiences more like those occurring in everyday life.

A second preliminary issue that should be reemphasised at this point is that lifelong learning is not confined to adulthood – otherwise it would not be lifelong. Nonetheless, most people spend far more of their lives as adults than as children, while most societies already make extensive provision for intensive learning experiences for children, to the maximum extent permitted by factors such as availability of financial resources. Thus adults constitute the major group of learners whose work would be facilitated by a system of lifelong education. Furthermore, since the present book concerns itself with the contribution of institutions of higher education to lifelong learning, our principal interest is, by definition, in adult learners and learning processes. By 'adult' we mean here simply anyone beyond the age limit defining childhood as it is understood in the society in question.

Prerequisities for lifelong learning

Of particular interest here are the psychological factors that influence adults' willingness to engage in a process of lifelong learning. This willingness to learn is affected by a group of *attitudes and values*: attitudes to learning itself, to themselves as learners, to particular learning, teaching activities and conditions, and to particular kinds of contents. To take a rather obvious example, adults who regard learning as a worthless activity, see themselves as unable to learn or regard the content of a particular activity as useless, would hardly be expected to show great interest in lifelong learning. On the other hand, those who see learning as an interesting and valuable activity leading to worthwhile results for their own lives, and regard themselves as competent learners, would be expected to display high levels of interest in lifelong learning. Thus preparedness on the part of adult learners is, to a considerable extent, a matter of possession of what might be called *personal prerequisites* for learning. As we have already mentioned, such prerequisites include attitudes, values and self-image.

In addition, however, the capacity for lifelong learning depends greatly upon what might be called *competencies or study skills*. Such skills would include the capacity to work without the direct supervision of a teacher (unless lifelong learning were to be supported by a system of lifelong schooling), knowledge about how to obtain information from outside sources such as libraries, the ability to set goals and devise strategies for achieving them, the capacity for assessing the extent to which such goals have been accomplished and to design alternative ways of pursuing them, skill in self-evaluation and so on.

The 'lifelong learner'

Taken together, these prerequisites define an idealised lifelong learner. Adapting the list developed by Cropley (1981), this individual:

1. is strongly aware of the relationship between learning and real life;
2. is aware of the need for lifelong learning;
3. is highly motivated to carry on lifelong learning;
4. possesses a self-concept favourable to lifelong learning;
5. possesses the skills necessary for lifelong learning.

The skills or competencies mentioned in item 5 include the following:

- capacity to set personal objectives in a realistic way;
- effectiveness in applying knowledge already possessed;
- efficiency in evaluating one's own learning;
- skill at locating information;
- effectiveness in using different learning strategies and in learning in different settings;
- skill in using learning aids such as libraries or the media;
- ability to use and interpret materials from different subject areas.

The influence of school

By the time higher education begins, many major learning experiences have already taken place in the home or in school. In fact, the influence of school is often negative: as von Bernem (1981) pointed out, many adults are actively inhibited from taking part in lifelong learning activities by unhappy experiences in the classroom. However, the inhibiting effects of schools are not confined to unpleasant memories: even a person who as a child experienced unbroken success in school may well have acquired habits and attitudes that are not conducive to lifelong learning. Among these are the idea that learning only occurs under the supervision of an authority figure, that success or failure is always externally defined, that the speed of learning or appropriate learning tactics are always specified by others, that all worthwhile knowledge is found in books and similar notions. In other words, even successful learners may acquire habits of passivity, or a one-sided view of what activities constitute worthwhile learning, while they may also fail to acquire appropriate knowledge and skills.

This implies that the school curriculum needs to be changed in order to promote growth of the personal prerequisites just listed. In an earlier paper (Cropley, 1979) it was emphasised that schools have a major role in fostering development of the ability and willingness to engage in lifelong learning. The 'action guidelines' that were spelled out there were designed with school curricula in mind, but many of them can be modified as guidelines for higher education. For this reason, a number of the objectives of instruction in the context of lifelong education are presented in slightly modified form in Table 3.1.

Table 3.1 *Objectives of instruction in the context of lifelong education*

Objectives related to:	
Vertical Integration	*Horizontal Integration*
Students acquire self-image as lifelong learners	Students regard learning in life as relevant to formal learning
Change produces positive motivation for further learning	Students are able to learn in a variety of settings
Students regard learning as an ongoing process	Students regard other learners as a valuable source of knowledge
Students gain experience in planning learning	Students are able to integrate material from different subject areas to solve problems
Students evaluate their own learning and identify necessary further steps	Students evaluate their progress in terms of broader societal criteria

Clearly, few existing systems of higher education would achieve all the objectives for vertical and horizontal integration listed in the table, but the goals cited here can serve as a set of criteria for lifelong education against which many of the innovative learning approaches described in later chapters may be judged. We shall consider these criteria again at various points throughout the book.

Implications for higher education

As we have just pointed out, the implementation of lifelong learning as a norm in a given society would require particular kinds of knowledge, skills, attitudes and values on the part of learners. It would also have to rest upon teaching and learning activities that departed from the norms of conventional classrooms. Institutions of higher education would thus have a three-fold function in helping to implement lifelong education. The first of these has already been outlined in Chapter 2: it would entail institutions' accepting a role as simply one element in a system of lifelong education, albeit an extremely important element. Secondly, institutions would also have an important part to play in promoting the development of the personal prerequisites and competencies for lifelong learning. This would be done partly by training people in lifelong learning competencies, and partly by providing them with opportunities to exercise skills they had already acquired. A major purpose here would be to equip people in such a way that they wanted to continue learning and believed they could do so. Thirdly, there is the special responsibility of teachers in higher education to serve as effective role models for lifelong learning. While this has importance in all disciplines, it is particularly crucial in the field of teacher education because of the obvious 'trickle down' effect on whole generations of potential lifelong learners.

The role of teachers

These roles may, however, clash with some of the more traditional functions of universities. Although the early universities were primarily teaching institutions, the members of the community of scholars were, by definition, experts in their subject areas, and hence the academy was a custodian and repository, as well as a purveyor of knowledge. Thus research in the sense of reflective inquiry has always been a characteristic of higher education, even though the tradition of scientific empirical research developed rather later – notably in the German universities of the mid-19th century. Most universities in the developed Western nations (plus a good many more outside this

47

geographical region) are active in research – both reflective and empirical – and teaching. A faculty member's duties at the University of Waterloo, Hamburg, or Harvard will normally involve some teaching and some research, plus the expectation of administrative service to the institution and possibly some type of service to the wider community. In many of the technical institutions much greater emphasis is placed upon teaching, in some cases to the exclusion of empirical research.

Concern with lifelong education and the promotion of lifelong learning skills in students, by contrast, implies the need for considerable faculty emphasis upon teaching methods and the organisation of instruction, yet in many institutions this requirement may conflict with the need for faculty to devote large amounts of time to research. This is a particular concern in an academic environment where the greatest professional rewards are accorded to accomplishments in scholarship and publication (as opposed to teaching and curriculum development). The situation is compounded further by the fact that in the great majority of universities the faculty have no preparatory training in methods of teaching and learning.

It is sometimes argued that the research activities of faculty are beneficial to their teaching, in the sense that active researchers are more up to date and involved. Unfortunately the empirical evidence suggests that this is by no means always the case (see, for example, Friedrich and Michalak, 1983; Linsky and Straus, 1975). It is not our purpose here to deny the value of university research or to argue against the involvement of university teachers in active scholarship. We merely wish to draw attention to an aspect of university roles and functions that places constraints on the time and attention that can be devoted to the encouragement of lifelong learning. We shall return to this question again in Chapter 6 when we discuss the role of instructional development activities in the promotion of lifelong education.

Students in higher education

Just as teachers in higher education may need to adjust to new roles that can better facilitate lifelong learning, it is also the case that the image of learning and learners that has been outlined above deviates from the profile of 'the university student' that is traditionally accepted. In nearly all cultures higher education has until recently been restricted to a narrow spectrum of the population – restricted in terms of age, social class, ethnic origin and often gender. Hence in many societies higher education has been confined to an élite group who went on to take leadership roles in government, business, and the arts. Attempts have been made in a number of nations, however, to change the definition of 'learner' in higher education, for example by such mechanisms as open admissions policies. Indeed, the types and numbers of students entering colleges and universities have changed dramatically in the past three decades.

The number of students receiving higher education has grown enormously in most developed (and many developing) nations, and this has led to the establishment of new universities and colleges, and to a huge expansion in the size of existing institutions. Additional student numbers were in part provided by the results of the 'baby boom' after World War II and partly by changes in admission policies. The great expansion of higher education from the late 1950s to the mid-1970s has now given way to a period of retrenchment in many parts of the world (Knapper, 1982), in which university enrolments have levelled or declined, new building has ceased, and university operating budgets have generally increased at a rate less than inflation. Taken together, these trends have resulted not simply in increased numbers of students in traditional age groups and taking conventional courses, but different kinds of students, sometimes learning in unconventional ways and settings.

Part-time students

During the late 1970s and early 1980s higher education has witnessed a marked change in the nature of the student body – though the trends we are about to describe have been far more prominent in some nations than others. The traditional time for higher education has been the years immediately after secondary school. Since study was generally full-time and often relatively costly, emphasis on the education of the young adult inevitably excluded other groups from the opportunity to participate in higher education.

Of course there were always exceptions to this generalisation. The tradition of university extension work goes back at least to the last century in many countries, with its aim of providing education to the surrounding community, often related to very specific vocational needs – for example the needs of local farmers. Departments of extension or continuing education were generally distinctive entities, with their own administrative structures, programmes and staff – although regular university faculty were often called upon to take part in teaching courses. Typically, programmes offered through extension were not for academic credit and were perceived – quite accurately – as quite different from the mainstream teaching activities of the institution. Indeed, Marriott (1982) points out that the extension movement as conceived in Victorian England was directed towards the moral improvement of the working class, without any intention of elevating working people in social rank: hence the rejection of diplomas and certificates and the stress upon 'disinterested' study that survives to this day.

While this impetus may in some ways be commendable (for example it gets around the problem of possible confusion between working for a qualification and learning something intrinsically worthwhile), traditional extension programmes have not been without their critics. For example, Hoggart, Stephens, Taylor and Smethurst (1982) have argued that, in Britain, there is a latent demand for continuing education that is not being fulfilled by traditional mechanisms. They echo the point made in Chapter 1 that rapid technological change has produced an urgent need for lifelong education – in contrast to the 'front-end loaded' model favoured by the higher education establishment (meaning provision of full-time courses for 18 to 21-year-olds). Hoggart and his colleagues make a further criticism that university extension departments suffer as a result of their status as separate units outside the regular academic programmes, and they call for the integration of continuing education with the routine work of teaching departments, where it can become the responsibility of all staff.

One way of increasing access to higher education is to offer opportunities for part-time study, whereby individuals might, for example, take courses while still holding a job. This apparently simple expedient is, surprisingly, extremely difficult in some university systems (for example in traditional British universities – see Hubert, 1989). In systems where programmes of study are compartmentalised into smaller course units, each awarding academic credit and evaluated separately, it is perhaps easier to accommodate students who wish to take only part of a programme. Hence part-time students have been relatively common for many years in North America, and indeed it has been quite usual to offer special courses to meet their needs – at night or in off-campus locations, frequently arranged under the auspices of the extension department. More recently there has been a growth of programmes – and even institutions – that cater specifically for part-time study: for example distance education programmes and open learning institutions, which we shall discuss further in Chapter 5.

Mature students

Part-time students are not merely different in terms of their patterns of attendance at college and university. Not surprisingly, such students have many other characteristics that distinguish them from the traditional full-time undergraduate. For example, they are frequently older, are more likely to hold full-time jobs, and more likely to be married and have children (Maslen, 1982). As mentioned above, so-called 'mature' students (usually implying in North America people who have passed their mid-20s and have discontinued formal education after secondary schooling) are not a new phenomenon in higher education. Many North American institutions have had special programmes for such students for many years; this often involves the waiving of normal admission criteria (perhaps with some type of aptitude test serving as a substitute). However, the great majority of such programmes typically have had the goal of assimilating older students into regular university degree courses: if any special provisions were made for mature students, these were likely to be in the nature of a modest counselling service that might give advice on choice of classes, help with study skills, and so on.

In the past few years, however, older students have been courted with increasing eagerness by some American colleges and universities, which have seen this group as a heaven-sent solution to the problem of declining enrolments among traditional-age students. In the United States the population of 18 to 24 year olds peaked in 1981, and it is for this reason that mature students are seen as a potential 'new market' for higher education. The American population is aging; the median age is now over 34, and by 2000 will be over 37, compared with a median of only 27 in 1970 (Ostar, 1981). In 1972, 29 per cent of students in American higher education were over 24 years of age. Six years later this figure had risen to 35 per cent, with about 70 per cent of those enroled part-time. During the past two decades part-time undergraduate enrolment increased much faster than that for full-time students: for example, in 1978 part-time undergraduate enrolment in publicly supported colleges and universities was 70 per cent greater than in 1970, while in private institutions there was a 25 per cent increase.

The crass appeal to 'find warm bodies to fill seats' overlooks the fact that this new student population may, as has already been pointed out, have substantially different learning needs from the traditional undergraduate. To cite just a few obvious examples, there is a need for much greater flexibility in the times and locations at which instruction is offered. Adult students may drop in and out of courses in a manner that is incompatible with an orderly, concentrated, and lock-step curriculum. Perhaps more important, the mature student may approach the learning process itself in a markedly different manner. Ostar (1981) comments that adult learners appear to be concerned about aspects of their lives that have not traditionally been regarded as 'academic' – emotional, interpersonal, spiritual and social factors.

Adults as learners

The whole topic of adult learning has, in fact, been the subject of a lively debate in recent years, characterised for instance by the assertion that the commonly accepted notion of declining learning ability in the adult years is a 'myth', and counter-claims that the belief that this is a myth is itself a myth (i.e. ability really does decline with age) – see Horn (1982) for a critical discussion.

It is clear that there are real differences in performance on learning tasks between adults and children, and also between older and younger adults. However, these differences should not be seen as a matter of presence or absence of a single, generalised learning ability before or after the conventional age for leaving school, but rather as embracing differences in the kinds of things that are most readily or least readily learned, the circumstances most favourable for promoting learning, the speed or efficiency with which certain kinds of learning are carried out, and the like. Even then, however, it is not clear whether these differences reflect purely or mainly changes in learning ability, or whether they are better regarded as reflecting differences in interest, motivation, and similar factors. In other words, it seems probable that differences in learning performance between people of different ages reflect special characteristics of learners and learning situations rather than, for instance, the onset of a fundamental inability to learn beyond certain age levels.

A number of studies have examined the ways in which adult learners differ from children (e.g. Boshier, 1977; Cross, 1981; Knox, 1974;

Wiens, 1977). Among the special characteristics of adults are that they usually bring to the learning situation more clearly developed personal goals, better formulated ideas about what constitutes useful subject matter, and a desire to learn things that they themselves (rather than a teacher) define as worthwhile, usually because these things can be applied in some way to relatively immediate real-life situations. As Knox (1974) perceptively noted, adults are seldom interested in learning answers to which they do not already know the questions. Adults are also affected by an unwillingness to be treated in ways that they regard as more appropriate for children, while they are more sensitive to 'social' factors such as fear of looking foolish in front of others or of being regarded as having developed snobbish inclinations. They typically have a low regard for abstract information but, perhaps paradoxically, tend to overestimate the importance of school learning and to underestimate the importance of non-school learning. They also frequently underestimate their own ability to learn in relatively formal settings. All of these factors combine to suggest that learning in adults is strongly affected by factors other than simply the ability to learn.

Gregor (1981) studied the special character of adult learners in relation to prevailing teaching practices in Canadian universities. University lecturers interviewed about their experiences with teaching mature students often reported frustrations and problems that seemed to combine both learning difficulties and attitudes. Gregor commented that many of the attitudes of adult learners were perfectly normal and reasonable, but they often provoked a defensive response in the instructors, who were attempting to maintain the 'adolescent learning' approach, which they were more used to. This in turn had the effect of discouraging mature students. Gregor condemned what he called the 'complacent lack of appreciation that there was in fact an issue: that adults do learn differently and should be approached differently' (p. 538).

Adult learning problems

From a psychological point of view, it is possible to identify a number of areas in which adult learners experience special difficulties in learning. These involve the cognitive domain (thinking, learning, memory), attitudes and values, motives, and self-image. Although the special cognitive characteristics of adult learners are of great importance, we will refer to them only briefly here, since they have been

53

described extensively by other writers (e.g. Poon 1980). To oversim-plify, memory becomes less effective, although this is partly a matter of decreasing ability to work at high speed and can be somewhat redressed by allowing more time for learning tasks. Strategies for storing information may also become less efficient as older people try to make new information fit into established categories. In principle this is a good thing, but it can impede learning in situations where the new ideas demand formation of new frameworks. Search and recall tactics similarly seem to become less effective. Since mature adults already have well developed cognitive structures and behavioural tactics for dealing with a wide range of events, they naturally seek to reapply these frameworks. Unfortunately, however, what they already know can easily interfere with their learning of new material. Thus older learners need more help than younger adults in structuring new information and avoiding inappropriate attempts to deal with genuinely new constructs in terms of preexisting structures. The well-known 'inflexibility' of mature adults is largely a result of such factors.

Turning to non-cognitive factors, it is apparent that in many Western European and North American societies there is a stereotype that older adults are largely incapable of learning; ('You can't teach an old dog new tricks.'). In the course of socialisation people learn the various roles appropriate to the society in question, so it is not surprising that many adults accept the role of the incompetent learner. This goes with the idea that schooling is something for children, a preparation for real life, so that it is a sign of being adult that one no longer goes to school. Furthermore, although this is often hard to grasp for teachers and academics who, by definition, fared well as students, many adults look back on their school years with distaste, even anxiety. School was for them a place where they were made to feel incompetent and where the instruction had little to do with the outside world of work and leisure.

Those adults who do pursue further formal learning opportunities study for a wide variety of reasons: for self-development, to make social contacts, to escape boredom, even to please others. But the most common motivation for learning is frequently external: to obtain the skills or knowledge needed for some special purpose, such as a job (Houle, 1961). Studies in both the United Kingdom (Stock, 1979) and the USA (Loring, 1978) showed that about half of all adult learning was carried out for such external reasons, and indeed, our discussion to date has mainly emphasised such reasons – the need for new skills and knowledge in the light of changing circumstances. Thus a substantial proportion of adult learners in a sense 'must' learn. Allied with the factors outlined above (changed cognitive abilities, negative attitudes to learning, problems with self-concept as a learner), this means that many adults enter learning situations with a good deal of anxiety. Anxiety in turn has known effects on cognition (selective attention, narrowing of interpretation of events, repetition of 'old' solutions, inability to break out of a stereotyped interpretation of a situation), and on emotions (feelings of humiliation, self-doubt, anger, projection of one's own negative feelings on to the teacher or the subject matter). These phenomena further increase anxiety, so that a vicious circle can develop – anxiety negatively affecting cognition and emotion, these heightening the anxiety, and so on. Thus adult students may face psychological difficulties in learning new skills that differ from the problems of 18 to 21-year-olds, and teachers need to take such factors into account when planning and delivering instructional programmes. On the other hand, many adults also have powerful internal motivations to study, an ability to link what they learn to their own experiences and learning expectations that are far more realistic than those of their younger counterparts. As many instructors of mature students will testify, teaching older learners can be an especially rewarding experience.

Special provision for mature learners

In essence, the argument here is for a new approach to teaching a more diverse population of students: what Knowles (1970) calls 'androgogy', in contrast to the traditional 'pedagogy'. The Canadian Association for Adult Education (1982) has called for greater attention to be paid to the development of teaching methods more appropriate to mature students. They point out that adult learners have often had previous negative educational experiences, and need special orientation, counselling and tutoring which is largely unavailable in traditional universities. For example, most educational institutions provide no opportunities for community or group learning, and fail to respond to the special problems that adults often bring to the learning situation. These include lack of encouragement from family and peers, poor study habits and a curriculum that is geared to adolescents.

A special challenge for higher education is the great diversity of abilities and characteristics that are represented by the new population of mature learners. Cross (1980) has pointed out that the basic approach to teaching and learning in higher education is to 'convene a group of students, pitch the content and pace to the mythical average student, and try to get them through a common course in the standard time of one semester' (p. 14). She mentions that the principal way in which traditional education handled this diversity was to permit vastly different levels of student achievement as indicated by a final grade.

Another, perhaps more prosaic, difficulty is that mature learners do not usually have the opportunity to spend as much time on campus, and hence the traditional university ambience (the 'community of scholars') is lacking for the commuting student. On the other hand, the fact that mature learners are deeply embedded in the outside world of work and community life provides splendid opportunities to provide horizontal integration by linking the school environment with concerns of the society at large.

A related limitation in the ability of traditional higher education to serve the needs of mature students is the fact that, until comparatively recently, universities and colleges have been in a seller's market, where the state provided funds to colleges and universities to dispense as they saw fit. Hence the prevailing approach to teaching has been to offer courses of instruction that seem appropriate to the teaching staff – the traditional custodians of the curriculum – as opposed to a strategy of assessing the real learning needs of a diverse population of students. In the past, state funding for higher education has usually been allotted directly to institutions, but recently there has been increasingly widespread discussion of alternative funding mechanisms – for example, the notion of giving government funds to individuals to spend where and when they see fit (as in the idea of educational 'vouchers', discussed again in Chapter 4).

At the same time as some commentators have been calling for more flexibility in accommodating mature students, others have stressed stricter admission criteria as a means of improving standards in higher education. This was the theme of a report of the United States National Commission on Excellence in Education, which was criticised by Keeton (1983). He argues that the correct goal for American higher education should be to improve teaching methods so that existing student populations can perform better and realise their educational potential. 'The Commission's remedies put the emphasis entirely upon the young students now coming of college age, not at all upon the much larger adult population of 23 years and older' (p. 2). The answer for

Keeton is not to tamper with the number of required days in school or required hours per day, but instead to look to the research on diverse learning styles and stages in adult development that might shed light upon the drive, motivation, clarity of commitment and goals of adult learners.

Academic difficulties of non-traditional students

Assuming that various measures do indeed encourage the enrolment of a broader range of students in colleges and universities, there remains the problem of dealing with the academic difficulties that many non-traditional students may encounter. As McCabe (1982) has written with respect to community colleges in the United States, these institutions 'have too often been more successful at enroling new populations than in serving them effectively' (p. 7).

Institutions have adopted a number of strategies for dealing with inadequate learning skills or academic preparation. The crudest is simply to introduce a rigid screening procedure at the end of the first year of study: here open admission is the equivalent of an opportunity to try – and if necessary fail. This type of screening on the basis of institutional examinations has been common for many years in higher education, especially with respect to prestigious professional programmes. At a time when many institutions face declining enrolments and increasing public calls for accountability, the waste of human resources involved in such approaches seems unacceptable.

A more positive approach to students with academic difficulties is to provide some type of compensatory or remedial education – perhaps coupled with a form of screening that, instead of 'weeding out' students with difficulties, diagnoses their problems and refers them to appropriate agencies within the institution for help. Remedial programmes typically cover basic skills (e.g. writing, mathematics) as well as the more general skills involved in studying at college or university. For example, the University of Waterloo requires incoming students to sit an English Language Proficiency Examination and, depending upon their performance, refers them to a Writing Clinic that provides one-to-one tuition in writing on a weekly basis for as long as it takes the student to pass the examination. Trow (1982) estimated that in 1979–80 the University of California spent over five million dollars for basic skills courses and programmes for underprepared students – and this figure excludes any calculation for the faculty time involved.

Sheffield University offers two-year preparatory courses for mature students involving what is termed 'flexi-study'. The latter includes packages of learning materials for self-study, teleconferencing, and 'surgery' tutorials. A similar approach is also taken in the 'Return to study' courses offered at the universities of Melbourne and Manchester. They are reminiscent of 'Outreach' programmes pioneered in the USA by institutions such as the University of Arizona. A variant of the same idea is to be seen in the Replan programme for the unemployed offered by Leeds University. This aims at helping such people analyse their situation and start working out ways of dealing with it by confronting feelings of inadequacy or low self-esteem. In a rather different approach to a similar problem, the University of Nottingham provides computer-based educational and training opportunities for disabled learners by means of electronic links to residential and day-care centres.

The various initiatives reviewed above have not been without their critics – for example on the grounds that it is not the function of universities to provide instruction that should have been completed in secondary school. However, it seems clear that if the basis of higher education is to be broadened by including students from different age groups with a much wider range of backgrounds, abilities and motivations, it cannot simply be taken for granted that they will all possess the appropriate skills to cope with university work. Indeed, many traditional students who have the formal entry requirement for higher education are deficient in academic skills. The question of appropriate study skills, both for traditional and non-traditional students, is taken up in more detail in Chapter 6.

Adapting course content for traditional students

Despite the foregoing comments, it would be a mistake to think that the best prescription for lifelong higher education is solely a matter of catering to mature students through special adult programmes, increased budgets for continuing education departments, more part-time learning opportunities, etc. To be sure, these are worthy initiatives, but they ignore the fact that a major clientele for higher education will continue to be the traditional full-time student entering college or university directly from secondary school. Laying the basis for lifelong learning among these individuals will thus be a major task for higher education – and one that will have important implications, not only for *how* people will learn, but also for *what* they will learn.

It is generally true that, in a rapidly changing world, content is often ephemeral, whereas learning skills themselves are applicable in a wide variety of situations that students may encounter after they have ended their formal university education (Lockwood, 1982). Nonetheless, certain types of knowledge and skills are probably essential foundations for later learning. Indeed the recent 'back to basics' movement in the United States attracted considerable publicity, and was perhaps an element in support of the renewed interest in core curricula stressing English language and numerical skills. Clearly, no-one will argue against the proposition that a student in higher education must be able to process verbal information (and in many instances mathematical information) in order to be a successful lifelong learner. However, if the idea of the basic curriculum is expanded to include a wide variety of other disciplines and content areas, then – depending on the teaching methods employed – there is a sense in which the whole endeavour may be counterproductive from the point of view of lifelong education. This is because of the danger that students may regard the curriculum as fixed and finite, and may lose the initiative to guide their own learning by selecting for themselves the relevant subject matters and appropriate skills most suited to their needs in later life.

In equipping students with the necessary abilities and motivation to tackle real-life problems there are at least two broad viewpoints within higher education. The traditional approach of universities is to have students master a certain body of information, as defined by a teacher or textbook, ultimately learn to extract what is relevant, and apply their knowledge to help solve real-world problems. A contrasting approach is to begin with a problem and have students try to solve it, working 'backwards' to acquire the necessary information and skills. We shall take up this theme again in Chapter 5 in the discussion of project work and independent learning methods.

Little (1983) points out the close parallels between Newman's definition of liberal education and the more contemporary goals of education spelled out in many university calendars and mission statements. When Newman's thoughts are translated into statements about course content, he can be seen as advocating that students acquire communication skills, ability in critical thinking, understanding of the local culture and differences between cultures, interpersonal skills (including empathy and tolerance), integrity and an ability to make

59

informed and responsible value judgements, as well as acquiring material necessary for working life and the ability to learn how to learn.

Cropley and Dave (1978) discussed various specific attempts to develop courses with lifelong learning itself as subject matter. In general, however, the practical experiences they reported indicate that such courses are not particularly valuable, because they do not foster the desired skills, habits, attitudes, motives and values. It seems far more likely that lifelong learning would be facilitated by changes in the orientation or organisation of existing content. As an example, they cited a college course in mathematics in which the contributions of various mathematicians were presented in a conventional manner, but were also related to life experiences of the scholars in question, societal trends of their time and so on.

Aalbeck-Nielson (1973) enunciated several principles for content which, although intended for school curriculum, are interesting in the present context. He concluded that the content of courses should be orientated towards themes such as time, space, and change. He did not suggest the adoption of special courses on these topics, however, but rather that they should be used as organising principles for the presentation of traditional contents in conventional disciplines. He gave a striking example of how to teach history with this perspective, and it seems probable that university teachers could successfully adapt many courses, even in strongly fact-oriented disciplines, along the lines he suggested. A study by the Unesco Institute for Education in Hamburg (Lengrand, 1986) has identified a number of areas that are thought to define the minimum content necessary in a system of education devoted to lifelong learning: these include knowledge of communication, science and technology, the fine arts, ethics and citizenship, time and space and, finally, how to care for one's own body.

In response to increasing concerns about degradation of the environment through pollution, global warming, disappearance of forests, extinction of plant and wildlife species, environmental education has been given great attention as one possible means of changing attitudes and behaviour. For example, the Government of Canada has introduced a 'Green Plan' that calls for more information about the environment and better environmental education 'to translate environmental awareness into action', with the object of 'creating an environmentally educated population' (Environment Canada, 1990, p. 9). In keeping with the principles of lifelong learning, the plan calls for education 'formally, through the school system, and informally, in the community, the workplace, and elsewhere'. The Canadian government has also proposed a Framework for Health Promotion in which education is seen as a major means of developing a new vision of health, in order to involve individuals and communities in the task of defining what health means to them and recognising that health is 'an essential dimension of the quality of our lives' (Health and Welfare Canada, 1986, p. 3).

It is not being suggested here that specific courses on the environment, health, ethics, and so on should become compulsory for all students, but rather that the themes in question should run through all courses and programmes, to the maximum extent possible. The idea that the principles and practices of effective learning have to be embedded in a broader curriculum and cannot be taught as isolated skills is a theme we shall return to later when discussing study skills and learning to learn.

Specialisation and integration: interdisciplinary studies

A different aspect of university and college teaching that relates to the goals of lifelong education is the question of specialisation and fragmentation of content, as opposed to integrating insights from a variety of disciplines. This is a concern within individual disciplines (see, for example, Solomon, Kavanaugh, Goethals, and Crider, 1982), within broader areas (such as the humanities, natural sciences, etc.) and across the entire curriculum.

Nearly all universities are organised along disciplinary lines, with teaching and research controlled by discipline-based departments. Professional rewards for teaching staff are also very much bound up with the discipline and department, and there is often little encouragement for lecturers who wish to collaborate with colleagues outside their home unit in, say, the team-teaching of an interdisciplinary course. Since personal prestige and success is very much influenced by scholarship and publication, it is of further significance to note that here too disciplinary ties are extremely strong. Trotter (1977) has commented that most university staff see themselves as owing first loyalty to their discipline, not the institution where they teach. He contends they see themselves primarily as physicists, lawyers or psychologists, and not as university teachers. This obviously serves to hinder cross-disciplinary collaboration, let alone true integration in teaching, especially since such values are undoubtedly communicated to students, both directly and indirectly. Nuttgens (1988) has argued forcefully against the dangers of being trapped by disciplinary boundaries, and went so far as to contend that certain disciplines only exist because they are taught in universities. He criticises a system of higher education which rewards those who are 'imprisoned in their disciplines, narrowed into their specialisms', while 'any real problems and any real innovation demand that we cross those boundaries and work together' (p. 121).

Many attempts have been made in higher education institutions to foster interdisciplinarity. In some ways the liberal arts curriculum, discussed in Chapter 2, is an attempt to combat undue specialisation. It is possible, however, that core curricula of this sort, while exposing students to a cross-section of courses, fail to take the further step of integrating ideas from a variety of disciplines, perhaps to show different approaches to a common problem. In this sense, it may be that disciplinary boundaries are paradoxically reinforced in the minds of many liberal arts students.

Some institutions have attempted to break down the disciplinary structures by employing organisational systems that are not based upon traditional departments. For example, both the authors were once on the staff of a Canadian university established in the mid-1960s with a curriculum and organisational structure that was intended to foster integration. Originally, all courses were offered within a single Faculty of Arts and Science; there were no departments as such, but 'divisions', including social science, fine arts, and so on. An attempt was made to recruit staff who could transcend disciplinary boundaries in their teaching and who believed in the set of goals spelled out for the institution. Within a few years, however, the university had reverted to an almost entirely traditional system of discipline-based departments, each with its own 'major' and distinctive curriculum. The divisions were abandoned, and even the Faculty of Arts and Science split into its two component parts. The reasons appear to be those mentioned above, stimulated by the infusion of increasing numbers of teaching staff with traditional values during the university's rapid expansion in the late 1960s.

This is not to say that interdisciplinary integration is impossible, or that all attempts to foster it are doomed to failure. Notable examples remain, ranging from the Faculty of Medicine at McMaster University, Ontario, to Roskilde University in Denmark, to Goddard College, Vermont. Many of the successful experiments include a curriculum that involves students in tackling problems rather than mastering traditional bodies of subject matter from particular disciplines. We shall examine some of these experiments and the factors determining their success in the next chapter.

Other approaches of a more limited nature include a requirement that students take part in an interdisciplinary course or courses (often at the beginning of their programme of study) but within the context of an otherwise traditional institution and discipline-based programme. One example of this type was the University of Keele's foundation year, in which first-year students worked on a set of issues or problems that, by their nature, transcended disciplinary boundaries. A similar approach is exemplified by the 'trunk courses' offered at Murdoch University in Western Australia, although these courses are not compulsory for all students, and also involve a major component that is aimed at teaching relevant study skills (see Chapter 6). A survey of tutor and student opinion about trunk courses (Educational Services and Teaching Resources Unit, 1982) showed both groups to be reasonably satisfied with the outcomes. It is interesting to note, however, that few of the students in the survey could point to ways in which their subsequent courses had built upon the interdisciplinary emphasis of the trunk course, and 90 per cent of the tutors said that they did not feel confident to teach a trunk course because of the many elements that lay outside their field of expertise; special difficulties were reported in teaching a mix of science and non-science students. Notwithstanding these reservations, both students and tutors liked the interdisciplinary aspect of trunk courses, as well as the contact with staff and students from other disciplines and exposure to new and unexpected material.

Despite increasing specialisation within many disciplines, there appears to be a growing recognition on the part of many academics that, as the information available to students in any particular field grows exponentially, the ability to integrate and maintain an overall perspective becomes critically important – perhaps even more important than mastery of specialised technical expertise. Beuret and Webb (1982) accuse engineering education in Britain of preparing students poorly in all but the most narrowly technical sense. They interviewed 250 graduate mechanical and electrical engineers and a further 200 of their colleagues working in a variety of organisations and industries. There was agreement that working engineers had little understanding of business practice, management skills, or company policy. Furthermore, the engineers were reportedly inept at communicating what they did understand to others in the organisation. The perceptions of colleagues were of special interest, and revealed a wide gap between what they would have liked the engineers to do and their actual capabilities. A major shortcoming was seen to be the engineers' inability to construe their work in a broad organisational context, and to describe engineering problems clearly to non-experts.

The researchers came to the damning conclusion that, overall, engineers tend to be 'intellectually and culturally isolated, partly because they find it difficult to see, or at least to treat seriously, any other perspective than their own'. The blame for this state of affairs is laid squarely on the shoulders of higher education. In particular, engineering departments are accused of placing far too much emphasis on technical subject matter in science and mathematics, and too little on practical experience of a broad range of problems – both engineering problems and management decisions. Some of the respondents admitted that they had ignored more broadly-based courses in order to concentrate on what they conceived as 'real engineering'. It came as a shock to them to find how little correspondence there turned out to be between the skills they had learned at university and those that were demanded of them in the work situation. It is interesting to speculate whether research of a similar nature in other professions would reveal comparable discrepancies between what is taught in university and the skills and attitudes necessary for work and for life.

In view of the dissatisfaction with a good deal of professional education mentioned above, it comes as no surprise that there have been calls to move away from specialisation. This was one of the recommendations of the Leverhulme Study Programme (Leverhulme, 1983), whose authors talked of the need to reduce undue specialisation, both in the secondary school system and in the early years of higher education. They pointed to the advantage of integrated degree courses in which students could be exposed to the methods and concepts of different disciplines. They also argued that the ability to integrate different ideas is justified not simply on philosophical grounds, but also has practical advantages, since jobs in future decades will require individuals who have the broad, general aptitudes that interdisciplinarity and integration imply.

The Leverhulme group's proposal to deal with this situation involved replacing the traditional British three- or four-year honours (specialised) degree programmes with a basic initial course of two years, or the part-time equivalent. They argued that a short initial and general course – providing there were possibilities for credit transfer between institutions, and entry requirements for subsequent courses were fairly open – would allow students the flexibility of tailoring higher education to meet their own particular needs and interests. Presumably too, students would not be locked into a premature choice of discipline, and perhaps career, as often happens in the present British degree system.

The idea of a two-year initial course at a general level that could subsequently lead to specialised training at a higher level is comparable to the system prevailing in many parts of North America where students enrol in a two-year programme – often in a community college – and then go on to take an undergraduate degree at university. The Leverhulme proposal was criticised in the United Kingdom, on the grounds that the two-year qualification would have low status and might be 'relegated' to certain institutions, leaving the more prestigious universities to continue offering traditional discipline-based education. A decade later the idea of a widely available two-year degree has been largely forgotten, though universities have moved towards more flexible programmes of study with increased possibilities for credit transfer and part-time attendance. Of more importance for our present purposes is the criticism that the Leverhulme recommendation spoke primarily to the question of content and organisation, rather than educational process. It seems to us rather naive to expect that the mere provision of a general programme would necessarily ensure the integration the study group values so highly. To achieve this would require changes in approaches to teaching and learning, which in turn would have to be based upon increased knowledge about the process of learning as well as flexible attitudes on the part of instructional staff. In fact, such concerns were voiced in some of the individual reports commissioned by the Leverhulme group (see Bligh, 1982), but the ideas raised here with regard to methods of teaching and assessment were not given the prominence they deserve in the final Leverhulme report.

The issue of teaching skills and attitudes is a key element in promoting lifelong learning within higher education, and is a theme that will be taken up again in Chapter 6. The difficulties of changing approaches to teaching are considerable, since in many instances – as touched on earlier in the chapter – the whole institutional reward system tends to downplay time and effort spent studying teaching and learning processes. Meanwhile, to cite the novelist John Gardner – education is to professors as water is to goldfish; they swim in it, but never look at it.

Recapitulation

Institutions of higher education that seek to implement the principles of lifelong education will be faced with making fundamental changes in their approach to teaching and learning practice. The changes indicated here do not comprise a complete list of all possible implications of lifelong education, but provide examples of the kinds of areas where practical changes might be profitable. In following chapters we focus directly on educational practice, rather than on an explication of theoretical constructs. These chapters are thus concerned with examples of reforms that would be needed in higher education institutions if fostering lifelong learning were to be adopted as a major goal. Chapter 4 outlines the kind of steps needed in principle, while later chapters turn to concrete examples that can be regarded as partial realisations of the various ideas outlined so far.

4   Lifelong learning and institutions of higher education

Transforming existing institutions

Lifelong education is sometimes understood as a synonym for a number of other terms, all of which have in common the notion of periodic renewal or refreshing of knowledge – for instance 'recurrent education', 'éducation permanente', 'further education', and as we have already mentioned, adult education. This tendency has been criticised in earlier chapters, and an attempt made to show that lifelong education has far more comprehensive implications than the 'synonyms' just listed. This is not simply a matter of words or labels. Equating lifelong education with recurrent education and the like can easily lead to the conclusion that it consists simply of the sum total of all institutions engaged in such activities. On the contrary, a system of lifelong education would encompass not only learning in such settings, but also in all settings – from formal to informal, from highly institutionalised to non-institutionalised. Nonetheless, the implementation of lifelong education would have important implications for educational institutions, and these are the subject of the present chapter.

It is unlikely that any society will simply scrap existing institutions and start again from the beginning, regardless of the degree of enthusiasm with which lifelong education is embraced. This means that its adoption would involve a transformation of existing institutions rather than the sudden imposition of something completely new. The nature of these transformations would be derived, naturally, from the principles of lifelong education that have already been outlined. It is impossible here to give a single universal blueprint for these transformations, just as it is also not feasible to list all desirable changes that could occur in higher education. However, general principles can be outlined, along with the questions, problems and dangers which then become apparent.

A transformation of institutions to achieve lifelong education raises a number of practical questions, which have been summarised by Kulich (1982, p. 136) as follows:

- Where and when is instruction to be offered?
- How are resources to be allocated?
- What content would be necessary?
- On what basis would certificates or credentials be issued?
- What teaching and learning methods would be appropriate?
- How would learners be financially supported?
- What new or altered support services would be needed?

To these may be added the question of how clientele would be selected. A number of these themes will be discussed in more detail in following sections. The intention is to provide a framework for presenting and discussing the various concrete steps that need to be taken in existing institutions of higher education, and which are to be described in later chapters.

Admission policies and procedures

Numerous attempts have been made in various countries to broaden the range of students attending college and university, using a variety of different mechanisms – financial, political, and social. It is important to bear in mind that general consensus about the importance of 'equality of opportunity' to enter post-secondary institutions can mask fundamental disagreements about who in society – and how many – can benefit from higher education. Hence there are very wide discrepancies between different countries in the proportion of school leavers entering university: in North America, for example, the ratio is at least double that of most Western European nations. Simply allowing more students into higher education does not in itself guarantee true equality of opportunity. Even in Canada, where almost half of eligible school leavers go on to university, this group is by no means representative of the general population, but rather is drawn disproportionately from upper socioeconomic groups (Anisef, Okihiro, and James, 1982).

The mechanisms for controlling who enters university vary from one system to another. Many European nations have public examinations, such as the General Certificate of Secondary Education in Britain, the French *Baccalauréat* or the German *Abitur*. In North America entrance requirements usually require successful completion of specified subjects in high school, depending upon the programme of study. Since high school marks are usually awarded by individual teachers, there are wide differences between schools, and some North American universities have their own clandestine systems for adjusting marks, based upon previous experience with undergraduates from the schools concerned. Furthermore the Scholastic Aptitude Test (SAT) is used widely in the USA as an important additional screening device for university admission.

Despite these differences in methods of student selection, many educational systems have in recent years been moving towards more open admission policies, in an attempt to recruit larger numbers and obtain a wider cross-section of students. There are at least three reasons for this trend. The first is philosophical, and is based on the egalitarian principle that all individuals in society should have the opportunity to enter higher education (even if they subsequently drop out). This is the spirit that guided the open admission experiment at the City University of New York, and the current open admission policies of many community colleges, such as the huge Miami-Dade Community College in Florida. The second reason, more pragmatic, is to increase the numbers and range of student intake in order to produce a more educated population and work force who can cope with the demands of an increasingly complex society. A final reason, also pragmatic and perhaps a little crass, is to accommodate – or reduce – excess capacity in institutions of higher education. For example, the report of the 1983 Leverhulme study of British higher education pointed out that British colleges and universities would have to adapt to the needs of new types of students if they were to avoid substantial excess capacity in the system (Leverhulme, 1983).

A combination of these reasons provided the impetus for changing admission standards, and helped stimulate the great expansion of higher education during the 1960s and 1970s. In the United Kingdom, for example, the Robbins report of 1963 proposed that the provision of places in higher education should be determined by the demand for qualified school leavers who were willing to enter degree-level courses. This rationale was accepted by subsequent national governments, and was the direct cause of the huge expansion in British higher education, including the establishment of many new universities and the creation of the polytechnic system. Twenty years later the Leverhulme Foundation sponsored the far-reaching study of higher education that has been referred to above. The final report (Leverhulme, 1983) addressed the question of access to higher education. While the authors welcomed the expansion of part-time and non-degree courses outside universities, they commented that the marked differences in participation rates between different social and economic groups – mentioned two decades earlier by Robbins – still remained. Indeed, they pointed out that in some ways the problem of equal opportunity had been exacerbated since the Robbins report. For example, Britain had become more ethnically diverse, and many minorities were poorly represented in higher education; the proportion of women students had risen but was still not equal to the rate of participation by men; and disparities persisted in participation rates between different regions of the country.

To quote another European example, Sweden embarked upon a radical and far-reaching reform of its educational system, beginning in the late 1960s. Important components of the reorganisation were a policy of open admissions, abolition of tuition fees (indeed generous provisions for additional economic support where necessary), and implementation of a system of recurrent education that was intended to provide opportunities for higher education at various intervals throughout an individual's life. The Swedish National Board of Colleges and Universities (Universitets-Och Högskoleämbetet) has been carrying out a comprehensive evaluation of the reform since it was initiated, but it is still not known how successful the changes have been in achieving the goal of democratising higher education and improving learning skills across the Swedish population. Certainly there is controversy among teaching staff in Swedish colleges and universities concerning the success of the reform, though it is not clear how much this is based upon objective evidence as opposed to a wistful desire to return to the halcyon days of the 1950s and early 1960s.

Unlike many European countries where higher education is coordinated in a unitary system and financed by the national government, the situation in the United States is much more diverse, with a wide range of types of higher education, sizes of institution, and financing arrangements. Hence it is not surprising that the move to more open admission standards has been piecemeal. Some radical experiments have taken place, and indeed are still continuing, as mentioned above. On the other hand, other experiments with open admission have been abandoned, including the one within the City University of New York. To oversimplify, the sudden change to a policy of admitting 'allcomers' threatened to overwhelm the system both organisationally and financially.

There are yet other difficulties with open admission policies. For example, certain specialised degree programmes, such as medicine, dentistry or architecture, are very much in demand, and are also extremely expensive. For this reason – and because most societies can employ only limited numbers of doctors, dentists, and architects – it is common to find limitations on entry to professional programmes, even where the general institutional policy may call for open admissions.

In the United States, in order to provide more equal opportunities for different ethnic groups, policies of 'affirmative action' were adopted that involved taking fixed quotas of minorities into certain programmes, despite the fact that they might have inferior academic entry qualifications. For example, Title IX of the Education Amendment, 1972, in the United States bars sex bias in federally assisted programmes and activities (Fields, 1983). Affirmative action has always been controversial, especially among students who feel they have been excluded from higher education by such policies. A well-known example was provided by the 'Bakke case' in which a student brought a successful action against the University of California at Davis on the grounds that he had been excluded from medical school when his academic qualifications were superior to those of other accepted students. The institution was compelled to admit Bakke to the medical programme (and in fact Bakke graduated in 1982).

Another, more recent, example of controversy surrounding changes in admission policies involves the reforms to higher education proposed by the French government, which were intended to allow initial entry to university for all students with a completed high school *baccalauréat*, while at the same time providing more rigid selection procedures at the end of the second year of study. The stated aim here was to introduce greater democracy into French higher education and to reduce class barriers, as well as to produce a larger number of skilled professional and technical workers. The reform generated violent opposition (including street riots) during the spring and summer of 1983 from both left and right wing student organisations. Students from the right protested that increasing access to fields such as law and economics would dilute the quality of education and lower the status of their degrees, while students from the left protested on exactly opposite grounds – that their choices of programmes would be more strictly limited by the selection procedures proposed after the second year (Dickson, 1983).

Teaching and learning activities

Many changes of a kind regarded here as desirable have already occurred in contemporary institutions of higher education. Yet many traditional elements of teaching and learning activities still predominate, often with negative effects for the implementation of the principles of lifelong education.

The predominance of the lecture

In Chapter 5 we shall review the rich variety of instructional methods in higher education that seem to us to be particularly appropriate for the encouragement of lifelong learning skills. These innovations should be seen, however, in the context of prevailing approaches to university and college teaching, which depend very heavily upon the lecture and, to a lesser extent, on the tutorial and formal laboratory. As Kozma, Belle, and Williams (1978) say in their comprehensive review of instructional techniques in higher education, 'For good or ill, the lecture hall remains the chief and usual meeting place for teachers and students' (p. 145). In similar vein, Eble (1972) concluded, on the basis of his study of 70 colleges and universities in the United States, that teaching in higher education primarily involves a single faculty member giving lectures to fairly large groups of students.

The lecture is one of the oldest types of teaching, and was used in higher education long before the development of the printed book. Indeed, in talking about the possible impact of information technology on higher education, some cynical observers have commented that the university may take the leap from oral to electronic transmission of information, having virtually ignored the use of print as a primary means for teaching. Clearly this is an exaggeration, and it is important to recognise that the lecture is only one component of a teaching method that involves the use of textbooks, library resources, and so on. Nonetheless, a great amount of time is spent by students listening to lectures, which in many institutions are regarded as the most important means of communicating information. The very title 'lecturer', which has widespread currency for university teachers all over the world, is perhaps an indication of what type of teaching is expected.

Indeed, the ubiquitous nature of lecturing appears to be so much taken for granted that there is a paucity of empirical evidence on the actual teaching methods used in higher education. One of the few studies that attempted to gather hard evidence about teaching approaches reported the results of a survey at a large metropolitan university in the United States with a population of 13,000 students and 400 members of faculty (Evans and Leppmann, 1968). Classroom lectures were ranked as the most used and most preferred teaching method by instructors, and ranked in second place by the students. More recently, Knapper (1990) found the lecture method was used by over 90 per cent of faculty he surveyed in two large universities in Canada and Australia. Evans and Leppmann conducted informal interviews at nine further campuses and were able to confirm their original results. They comment (pp. 56-57) that their results 'indicate a preference by professors for those methods which cast the university teacher in his traditional role: standing before the class, giving a lecture, using the blackboard, assigning some outside homework, and occasionally giving a classroom demonstration . . . the students pretty much agreed with their professors about these methods'.

Despite this apparent satisfaction with traditional methods, criticism of the lecture technique has existed since the middle ages (Kozma, Belle, and Williams, 1978). Arguments against the lecture are that it involves a passive approach to learning, and is largely out of the control of the student. Such criticisms have some support from empirical literature about the effectiveness of the lecture in comparison with other teaching methods. Bligh (1972) summarised the results of a large number of studies on the effectiveness of lectures for several different goals, including the acquisition of information, promotion of thought, and changes in attitude. On the basis of his comprehensive analysis he concluded that the lecture can be about as effective as other methods (e.g. classroom discussions) for transmitting information, but that for achieving higher level conceptual skills most lectures are not as effective as active learning methods, and lectures are relatively ineffective for changing attitudes or fostering personal or social adjustment in students.

From the point of view of our interest in promoting lifelong learning skills, Bligh's findings on what he calls 'the promotion of thought' are of particular significance. He comments (p. 33) that:

if students are to learn to think, they must be placed in situations where they have to do so . . . The best way to learn to solve problems is to be given problems that have to be solved . . . If this thesis seems obvious common sense, it should be remembered that some people place faith in their lectures to stimulate thought and expect thinking skills to be absorbed, like some mystical vapours, from an academic atmosphere . . . Learning to think is not an absorption process.

Bligh even takes issue with the conclusion of Evans and Leppmann, reported above, that the lecture is a popular teaching method for students. Citing evidence from several British studies, he concludes that on the whole lectures are less popular with students than other more active approaches. Lindquist (1978b) supports this contention, and goes further to point out that the very size, impersonality, and traditionalism of many universities in the United States has led to student disenchantment with their teaching. Lindquist carried out surveys of students on a number of campuses and found that many of them believed their teaching to be 'too uniformly didactic', their learning 'too passive', and their teachers often too 'soporific'.

Despite this indictment, Bligh and Kozma *et al.* are forced to admit that getting faculty to change from the lecture method (either by adapting it to allow for more student interaction or by replacing it with other, more active teaching methods) often meets with considerable faculty resistance. It is often argued that the lecture is inexpensive, since it rarely involves equipment costs and allows a single teacher to address large numbers of students simultaneously. The lecture also makes fewer demands on the instructor's time, both in terms of interacting with students and in preparation for teaching, compared to, say, project-based learning (discussed in Chapter 5). It seems likely, however, that the lecture has retained its prominence simply because it is the method that university teachers were themselves exposed to as students. Since a great majority of university lecturers receive no instruction in methods of teaching and learning, it is hardly surprising that they use the only role models available to them from their own higher education.

Laboratory instruction

While most concern about traditional teaching methods in higher education has focused upon the lecture, the formal laboratory too is not without its critics. Elton (1983), for example, has discussed the high costs involved in teaching practical work in laboratories, and has also summarised the dissatisfaction with the method that has been expressed on both sides of the Atlantic. A major concern here is that student work in the laboratory frequently gives a false impression of how science is carried out, how problems are solved and discoveries made. This is thought to be because of the artificial constraints within the laboratory – the need for students to work on set exercises within limited time periods. All too often an undue emphasis is placed upon the importance of getting the correct result, as opposed to the process of investigation, and the impression is given that science is a neat, cut-and-dried means of arriving at elegant solutions. Pickering (1980), in a provocative article in the *Chronicle of Higher Education*, asked whether lab courses were a waste of time, and this provoked a lengthy and sometimes vituperative correspondence in the *Chronicle's* subsequent issues. One correspondent, in an ironic defence of the formal laboratory, justified the method as part of a long-standing religious ritual in science teaching. McConnell, in his 1980 presidential address to the Division on Teaching Psychology of the American Psychological Association, presented a wry but disturbing account of his experiences as a distinguished professor who returned to the classroom to study medicine at the University of Michigan, and encountered at first hand the problems of coping with the weekly lab. Among the many problems revealed by McConnell's account was the frequent failure of lecturers to be aware of the real learning processes at work in the laboratory, and the discrepancy between the learning that took place and the instructional aims for practical classes. This situation is often exacerbated by the lack of frequent and careful liaison between the course instructor and the laboratory demonstrators who run the labs and are frequently drawn from the ranks of graduate students (McConnell, 1980). Boud has written extensively on the laboratory method, has reviewed a wide range of approaches to lab teaching, and made recommendations for changes that might make the laboratory a more effective learning device (see Boud, Dunn, and Hegarty-Hazel, 1986).

The special problem of professional education

The efficiency of traditional teaching methods has been a particular concern within professional higher education, where the defects resulting from inadequate preparation appear quite quickly and distinctly once graduates embark upon their careers. For example, dissatisfaction has been expressed with medical education, especially its emphasis on scientific and medical detail (taught primarily through lectures) as opposed to clinical skills learned through practical experience. A panel established by the Association of American Medical Colleges commented in 1982 that the 30 to 40 hours a week of traditional classroom learning during the first two years of medical school might be of little value, since much of the information transmitted may well not be used. Similar concerns were reported by a Presidential Commission for the Study of Ethical Problems in Medicine and Biomedical and Behavioral Research, which suggested that medical schools should try to improve students' communication skills and ability to work with patients, as opposed to encouraging rote learning (McDonald, 1982).

Wallis (1983) reports that medical school deans and members faculty are increasingly expressing disquiet about producing narrow-minded graduates who have little perspective on the facts they have memorised – facts that are in danger of overwhelming the learner, despite the fact that they contribute little to successful medical practice. Comparable criticisms have been made about medical education in West Germany, where a great deal of learning consists of 'piecemeal acquisition of unrelated, detailed, factual subject matter' (Kloss, 1982). Kloss regrets that due to the vast number of medical students in Germany more active types of learning (e.g. in small tutorial groups) have become virtually non-existent, and he claims that many students have never had the opportunity to examine a patient.

Turning to a different type of professional education, Broderick (1983) surveyed 300 Honeywell managers from throughout the corporation in an attempt to gain insights into the type of education and training they had received and its relevance to their current management tasks. He found that only a small fraction of an individual's management techniques had been learned in the classroom, and he estimated that perhaps 80 per cent of real learning came from contact with other people and on-the-job experience. Somewhat similar conclusions were reached by Howard (1986) in a longitudinal study of the relationship between college experiences and managerial performance at AT&T.

Role of instructors

Achieving radical changes in teaching and learning activities would depend to a considerable degree upon acceptance of an altered role for instructors in colleges and universities. For example, in a system of lifelong education teachers would be seen more as guides or helpers than as authoritative sources of all knowledge. It might also be expected that they would make more frequent use of practitioners or experts, especially people from real-life settings where the knowledge and skills being transmitted find their application. Another possibility is that instructors and students could work together in areas where neither are expert. This was the basis of the University of Keele's 'Foundation Year' in which small groups of staff and students explore topics that lie outside the teacher's own expertise. This approach has been adopted in other British universities, as well as in universities elsewhere in the Commonwealth, such as Zambia. Finally, if university teachers are to function effectively as lifelong educators, they themselves would have to engage in a process of lifelong learning. Of course the role of lifelong learner is, at least in principle, in no way novel for teachers in higher education, since part of their professional responsibility is to conduct research or at least to update continually their knowledge of the discipline. Nonetheless, it is quite possible that many staff members would reject any conceptualisation of their role and duties that reduced their authority.

In commenting at length on the need for more student-centred learning, The Leverhulme Programme of Study into the Future of Higher Education emphasised the concomitant need for flexibility in approaches to teaching (Bligh, 1982). Goodlad, Pippard, and Bligh (1982), in a paper on curriculum for the same study, talk about the need to produce 'authoritative uncertainty' in students, and to stress 'action-oriented' thinking based upon practical, real-world learning experiences, as opposed to passive learning approaches. A key question here is whether faculty will be prepared to give up their traditional role as experts and instead become facilitators and mentors, helping students to take a more active role in directing their own learning. Heerman, Enders and Wine (1980, p. 9) comment that 'at the heart of the matter is the question of whether the traditional roles of the classroom teacher and the campus will change in response to an emerging generation of learners and learning needs which are neither sequential, predictable, nor orderly in the manner to which educators have become accustomed'.

Academic attitudes

It seems plausible that a key factor in the introduction of lifelong learning in higher education is the attitudes of teaching staff (see, for example, Nordvall, 1982) and the need to change preconceptions about educational goals and methods. Faculty resistance to change often reflects a general conservative attitude among the professions, with a tendency to prefer known methods (Evans, 1968). In the profession of teaching, the role model is frequently cautious and traditional, and – as we have pointed out earlier – is not modified by training, since university graduate schools pay virtually no attention to methods of teaching and learning (Gaff, 1978). Indeed, in graduate training, loyalty to the discipline is generally presented as of more importance than teaching the discipline (Hefferlin, 1969).

In this connection, Cahn has argued that those in charge of graduate programmes 'have the responsibility to provide courses in methods of teaching for students intending to enter the profession. And these courses should be required of all to be recommended for teaching professions' (Cahn, 1978, p. x). One innovation along these lines was the Doctor of Arts degree in the United States, in which students not only specialised in a discipline but also studied the teaching of that discipline. Although the degree still exists in a handful of American universities, it has not succeeded in having the impact on graduate training that was hoped for by its originators. This seems to be partly due to the greater prestige of the traditional Ph.D. degree, but also to the reduced opportunities for doctoral graduates to enter the academic profession because of declining student numbers and university budgets.

Stiles and Robinson (1973) have commented that, since teaching is regarded as a highly independent and personal pursuit, lecturers tend not to be exposed to the ideas of colleagues, and may be reluctant to adopt new approaches. Indeed, adoption of ideas used elsewhere may even be a tacit admission that teaching can somehow be 'standardised', which may in turn lead to the notion that it is possible to rely on package courses, and teaching by television, without the need for the individual control of instructional situations that many professors value very highly (Hefferlin, 1969). It can also be argued quite plausibly that change for its own sake is not necessarily a good idea, and hence some resistance may be perfectly logical.

Certainly faculty attitudes towards innovation can be inhibiting to someone who wishes to experiment with a new approach. Innovation may provoke antagonism from colleagues who interpret the change as an indirect criticism, and hence few instructors find it easy to adopt teaching practices that are radically different from those of their colleagues (Cohen and Brawer, 1977). The influence of traditionalism is strong. 'There is a reassuring simplicity in the old ways of teaching. They may not work well, but they are a solid tradition to fall back on ... The irony of this order is not simply the static knowledge it produces, but also the alienation it provokes' (Shor, 1980, p. 22).

In contrast, Bruenig (1980) has commented that anticipation of faculty resistance to change may be a self-fulfilling prophecy. He argues that, with some encouragement, staff involved in an innovative project that he studied were in fact willing to improve their performance, and he traced these attitudes to their high level of education, idealism, sense of vocational stability, professional interests and exposure to the optimism of their students. Failure to embrace innovation may also be due in part to lack of information about alternative methods. For example, in a comprehensive study of teaching at the University of Alberta, department heads reported a great many teaching innovations, yet they were largely unknown to colleagues in other academic units (Knapper, 1988a). It remains true, however, that academics in general tend to place high value on objective evidence, and the beneficial results of educational innovations are often hard to pinpoint precisely (Sikes, Schlesinger, and Seashore, 1974).

Evaluation and certification

If only to facilitate student transfer from one institution or department to another, it seems inevitable that a system of lifelong education will have to make appropriate provision for examination and certification of student achievement. Indeed, Pineau (1980) has made the point that certificates, even of a relatively traditional kind, would continue to be important in a system of lifelong education. This is because a mechanism to certify that certain learning has occurred makes the knowledge 'portable'; without such certification, the danger exists that new knowledge and skills acquired in the course of lifelong learning would be negotiable only in the precise setting where the learning took place. A concrete example of the problem of certification is the difficulty being experienced by 'open entry' programmes in assigning credit for learning taking place outside traditional institutions.

It is also important to note that formal qualifications in the form of certificates, credits, etc. are not only important for the purposes of educational institutions, but that learners themselves are eager to obtain some kind of paper qualification. This is because they are aware that a certificate or similar tangible result of some learning activity can lead to job advancement or other material advantages. As Cropley and Dave (1984) pointed out in a summary of several studies on in-service training of teachers, potential clients are keenly interested in the question of whether or not a particular learning activity culminates in some kind of examination or other formal evaluation, because they have learned in the past that 'serious' learning activities are usually concluded in this way. Students usually want to take part in learning activities that are academically respectable, and they equate respectability with a formal evaluation. Activities that yield a certificate or other document based on an exam are thus regarded as especially worthwhile.

The tradition in higher education

The provision of portable qualifications, 'credentialling', is a function which is familiar to institutions of higher education. While teaching is perhaps their major activity, an equally important, related task involves the certification that learning has taken place. The role of colleges and universities in granting appropriate credentials to graduates has a very long tradition in higher education and operates through the award of degrees, diplomas or certificates. In North America most institutions go further by awarding credits for each component (course) that makes up a programme, and in many instances these credits have a 'value' and may be transferred to another institution. The credentials awarded by universities in some instances constitute quite specific licences to enter and practise a profession – as in the case of architecture, medicine, engineering, etc. Other qualifications are less closely tied to particular professions or careers, and yet in practice may be used by employers as indicators of general competence and possession of minimum require- ments for positions within an organisation. The credentialling role of higher education is thus of major importance for society at large, since it serves as a screening mechanism for a very wide variety of occupations. Indeed, the great importance attached to this activity is indicated by the fact that in the United States, for example, there exists a complex mechanism for accrediting the various institutions that provide credentials – the so-called accreditation agencies that ensure the *bona fides* of colleges and universities within each state.

Criticisms of existing practice

Despite this traditional role of higher education, the value of academic qualifications for predicting occupational competence has frequently been called into question. For example, North American research has shown repeatedly that the relationship between college grades and success in a profession is extremely small, and that the overall variance accounted for by grades makes them almost useless in predicting occupational effectiveness or job satisfaction outside certain occupational settings such as the armed forces (Cohen, 1983; Samson, Graue, Weinstein, and Walberg, 1983).

At a conference on American higher education sponsored by the Association of American Colleges in 1982, criticisms were heard that the *baccalauréate* degree had become an almost meaningless credential that was not serving the needs of society (Scully, 1982). Degree programmes were attacked as lacking coherence, and the view was expressed that the paper qualification needed for job entry had become far more important than the quality of learning taking place. The conference was part of a three-year-long project to investigate 'quality and coherence in *baccalauréat* education', and there was agreement on a set of skills it was felt someone with a bachelor's degree should possess. These included the ability to reason critically, write and speak clearly and cogently, understand the individual's role as a citizen and function effectively in society, make appropriate ethical and aesthetic judgements, understand other cultural perspectives and understand some of the social and economic issues raised by scientific and technological developments. It is interesting that this list quite closely resembles some of the prescriptions for appropriate lifelong learning skills discussed in earlier chapters.

In fact, however, it is in the area of student assessment that perhaps the greatest discrepancy arises between stated goals and actual effects of teaching and learning activities. When asked about their aims for a particular course, university level teachers will frequently mention higher order learning skills, such as analysis, synthesis, creativity and critical thinking (see, for example, Thorp, 1981). In practice, however, an examination of the tasks students are asked to perform in many courses (examinations, tests, assignments) reveals that the learning involved may often be at a much lower level, perhaps requiring simple memorisation of facts (see, for example, Milton's witty critique of examination procedures in higher education, *Will that be on the final?* – Milton, 1982). Farago (1982) also indicts the conventional grading system for discouraging students from pursuing independent, idiosyncratic educational goals. He admits, however, that students themselves may prefer a finely discriminating grading scale that enables them to compete successfully in the job market. Whether or not that is true, some empirical support for Farago's criticism of assessment practices comes from a study by Watkins (1984). In a longitudinal study of students at a major Australian university he found that most approached learning in a shallower way at the end of their programme than on entry. He attributed the change largely to the fact that most assessment tasks appeared to discourage 'deep' learning. Similar findings were reported for Hong Kong students by Gow and Kember (1990).

A more extreme interpretation of present practices regards modern universities simply as 'credentialling factories' competing in the marketplace for student 'consumers', and argues that academic staff have forfeited the right to be the primary custodians of the goals and content of higher education (Farago, 1982). Other relevant factors mentioned by Milton (1982) as encouraging poor examination practices include the preponderance of multiple-choice tests supplied with many standard textbooks, and the fact that so much testing of students in North American universities is left to teaching assistants who receive no training in the purpose and practice of evaluation of learning.

Elton (1982) explains the 'quite unreasonable stress on low-level abilities' in much examining by reference to the knowledge explosion and the difficulty of devising assessment tasks that test relevant and useful skills, especially in the science areas. He goes on to say that, nonetheless, 'teachers must search their consciences and discover whether they really want to produce walking encyclopedias rather than active human beings' (p. 117). Elton calls for a system of assessment that is less stressful than the final examination system used in most British universities, and which is also more relevant to the knowledge and skills needed for real life. This would include a move towards the use of self- and peer-assessment by students which, he argues, would help to develop student autonomy in learning. Elton points out, however, that to achieve such changes will be difficult given the attitudes and level of understanding of many members of faculty with respect to the underlying philosophy and psychology of learning evaluation. He ends with a recommendation that teachers in higher education should receive formal training related to student assessment.

Kloss (1982), in his critique of German medical education, mentioned earlier, reports particular dissatisfaction with the examination structure. He points out that most of the final state examination in medicine consists of multiple-choice tests; there is in addition a brief oral examination, but this, according to Kloss, does not reflect the students' experiences during the practical year. Reforms in medical education in the 1970s (the *Approbationsordnung*) were intended to make the learning experience more practical, to foster closer contacts between medical students and patients and to introduce some new subjects, such as sociology and psychology. Kloss maintains, however, that the efforts have been virtually nullified by the examination system being used. He reports that written exams test factual knowledge in a disjointed manner, fail to evaluate students' clinical skills in dealing with patients, and do not allow students to demonstrate their ability to apply theoretical knowledge. An 829–page subject/content catalogue provides a detailed listing and classification of the medical curriculum and, says Kloss, encourages students to learn factual information by rote. Student study is guided by these catalogues (and textbooks based upon them), so that only parts of the course that are directly linked to the multiple-choice examinations are attended to. 'Because it is possible to pass with only a certain (variable) percentage of correct answers, whole areas, including even medicine or pathology, can be neglected and the candidate can still be successful' (Kloss, 1982, p. 10).

The subject/content catalogue and related multiple-choice examination questions constitute what Snyder (1971) has referred to as the 'hidden curriculum', which may have little resemblance to the formal course requirements as laid out in high-flown statements of objectives specified in course outlines and departmental calendars. Students are often extremely adept at pinpointing what is *really* required to do well in a course, based upon subtle cues from the instructors when they talk about assessment procedures, on inspection of previously used tests, conversations with former students, and so on (Becker, Geer, and Hughes, 1968; Kuh, 1981; Snyder, 1971).

Student success at disentangling the hidden curriculum may be reflected in high marks, but these grades may be a poor reflection of the higher level problem-solving and critical-thinking skills that are generally associated with effective lifelong learning. Hence it is not surprising that, as mentioned earlier, academic grades are poor predictors of success and satisfaction in many careers. Indeed, Heath (1977) showed that college grades and even receipt of college honours were not found to predict measures of adult maturity and competence – if anything, the reverse held true. This seems to raise serious questions about customary methods of teaching and assessing student performance in higher education.

Although formal qualifications could not simply be rejected out of hand in a system of lifelong education, for reasons stated earlier in this chapter, it is thus imperative that they take on different forms from those that predominate at present. The question of certification has been discussed from the point of view of lifelong education by Pflüger (1979): he argued that certificates should describe not what level in a system has been reached or what formal examinations have been successfully negotiated, but rather what knowledge and skills have been obtained. For instance, the certificate might refer to a catalogue, in which the things the student has actually learned to do were listed, rather than simply giving the title of an exam which had been passed. Assessment might also be seen as 'formative' rather than 'summative'. In other words, certificates and the like might provide a profile of strengths and weaknesses which could be used to plan further learning activities, rather than offering a statement that a particular number of points had been obtained.

Practical difficulties and problems

Achieving coordination among institutions

A crucial idea in lifelong education is that valid educational opportunities exist outside traditional institutions. One major issue for existing formal institutions of post-school education would thus be how to achieve coordination with the complex array of educational opportunities existing 'outside'. This problem is not simply one of organisation (for example ensuring that timetables do not conflict) but is also, to a considerable degree, a social-psychological matter. For instance, formal post-school education as it is offered in universities is traditionally regarded as superior to non-formal education, while employers typically define job qualifications in terms of courses and certificates acquired in traditional institutions. Integrating and coordinating all forms of post-school education would also raise crucial questions in the area of decision making. Universities, for example, would be reluctant to give up any of their independence, or to sacrifice their right to be the sole arbiters of what is academically worthwhile and what is not. Many university staff members could be expected to be loath to accept new definitions of competence, or to work side by side with practitioners who may have limited formal qualifications and no research experience. Issues of this kind mean that traditional institutions of higher education would be confronted by problems not only of a straightforward management kind, but also by issues of status and power.

Although status and power would be important, it is clear that practical matters too would have to be dealt with. Many of the forms of post-school education now in existence would presumably have to be coordinated with each other, and each already has its own philosophy, goals, forms of governance, financing arrangements and jurisdictional basis. Thus, rationalisation of financing, development of policy, hiring and firing of staff, administration and provision of leadership and the like, would all raise special difficulties. At present, virtually no knowledge exists about how to organise a system of education encompassing both formal and non-formal institutions, although in the United States the Council for the Advancement of Experiential Learning has begun to address such issues in ways that will be touched upon in Chapter 5.

One possible administrative/management strategy that might be adopted to foster cooperation among colleges and universities is the exchange of personnel between institutions. For instance, a professor of mechanical engineering might spend a period working with future Industrial Arts teachers. Another possible mechanism for facilitating cooperation among different kinds of institutions involves what Walker (1980) called 'adhocracies'. For example, personnel from industry and commerce could work on a short term basis with university or college staff to develop a particular programme. Not to be forgotten in this process are members of the communities in which the institutions concerned are located. Indeed, involvement in decision making of learners themselves as well as members of the community at large is an important principle in lifelong education, and one that seems capable not only of facilitating coordination between different kinds of institutions, but also of helping to strengthen links between institutions and the wider population. Of course, many activities along this line already exist. Adoption of lifelong education would not necessarily involve implementation of previously unheard of measures, but rather a strengthening, expansion and improvement of existing procedures.

Administrative constraints

Within individual institutions many administrative difficulties may be expected to arise. Yet despite these superficial differences, there are often considerable similarities among institutions in such matters as the division of departments and faculties into disciplines; the time needed to complete a degree (in terms of years of study; the number and length of terms per year; the number of courses per term, and so on). Innovative teaching practices that do not mesh with these administrative arrangements will face considerable obstacles to their implementation. Within national boundaries there is an even more remarkable similarity in administrative structures. Indeed, in North America the credit transfer system virtually demands it. The fact that this may represent a confusion between 'class contact hours' (what elementary school teachers call 'seat time') and the amount of student learning that actually takes place (largely outside the classroom, even in the most traditional of courses) does nothing to ease the burden of an innovative teacher who wishes to experiment with a new instructional approach.

For example, many relevant teaching methods, such as project-based instruction, do not easily fit into a schedule that requires a class to meet for three separate hours each week over thirteen weeks. Field-based teaching, to cite one instance, may depend upon students devoting concentrated blocks of time to learning that takes place far from the physical structure of the campus, and this may well conflict with the demands placed on students by other, traditional courses. In any case, simply 'putting in time' in the classroom may not result in the most effective study, and there is some evidence that heavy student workloads can result in shallower learning (Ramsden and Entwistle, 1981). Furthermore, in the light of rapidly increasing knowledge in most academic fields, it is increasingly unrealistic to achieve comprehensive content coverage. Hence some universities have actually moved to reduce formal course requirements while trying to enhance the quality of the learning experience for students. For example, at the University of Waterloo degree requirements in science, mathematics, and engineering were changed in the late 1980s to reduce the number of required courses. Paradoxically, in the case of mathematics this resulted in student protests that the value of their qualifications was being compromised (*University of Waterloo Gazette*, 1989).

Changing approaches to student assessment may also present difficulties for institutions that specify a range of possible grades from A to F, calculate grade point averages to two decimal points, and have the tacit expectation that all instructors will provide a set of marks that are elegantly distributed along a normal curve. It will be seen, for example, that many of the innovations described in Chapter 5 are based upon the concept of 'mastery learning' and the achievement of certain minimum learning criteria in order to guarantee a satisfactory mark (what is known as 'criterion-referenced testing'). This produces skewed grade distributions that tend to disturb department heads and registrars – even though in many cases the results of assessment are completely in accordance with the predictions of educational theory. In the case of some other learning approaches it is regarded as desirable for students to act as assessors, by grading themselves and perhaps their fellow students. This is quite consistent with the way assessment is frequently conducted in non-academic work settings. Once again, however, it is likely to conflict with academic institutional norms.

Even institutional location and architecture can compromise certain educational methods and goals, and it is interesting that some innovative universities (such as Roskilde) have designed environments that break away from the traditional model of small seminar rooms and large classrooms with fixed tiers of seats – and often the ubiquitous laboratory bench, complete with gas pipe and sink at the front of the room. Hummel (1977) presents a number of examples of school design that he argues are more suited to lifelong learning concepts (such as the open classroom). We are talking here, however, not merely of physical structures but of a whole administrative ambience that guides the way teaching in higher education is organised. As McCabe (1978) comments, 'Nothing can be more frustrating than for faculty to develop a well-conceived and economically feasible plan for learning, only to find that their management systems are not designed to accommodate it'.

Financing

Yet another obvious constraint on innovation involves costs. It is frequently the case that departures from the traditional require extra financial resources – not only to initiate the new approach, but also to provide evaluative evidence that the innovation is successful compared to existing teaching methods. On the other hand, many innovations may actually save money. Savings in instructional costs for the institution itself have been the impetus for a variety of new approaches to teaching and learning, including individualised instruction and various types of instructional technology, reviewed in Chapter 5 (although the financial outcomes in many cases have been disappointing). In the longer term, if new methods are indeed successful in producing more effective learners who can operate more efficiently throughout their lives, then the general benefits to society – including financial benefits – are obvious. But this is small comfort to university administrators who must cope with fixed – or even declining – budgets at a time of general fiscal constraint. Hence the proponents of lifelong education are faced with the extremely difficult challenge of demonstrating the longitudinal benefits of the changes they advocate.

The whole issue of financing can also be looked at from the point of view of individual learners. The ability to take advantage of higher education is limited by the costs involved, both direct (e.g. tuition fees) and indirect (e.g. loss of earnings while studying). Some nations, including Sweden, Australia, and West Germany, have experimented with abolition of student fees entirely, and many countries provide student loans or, more unusually, outright grants (the latter generally calculated by a means test). However, this may not be sufficient inducement for some potential students, who would have to face a reduced standard of living, and disruption in their careers in order to take advantage of higher education. More radical means for encouraging participation in higher education by adults already in the work force include the extension of the notion of 'sabbatical leave' for workers, coupled with free tuition and paid educational leave, exemplified by the Swedish concept of partial salary.

In discussing the issue of financing lifelong education, Kurland (1980) has made two suggestions, both involving 'mixed' approaches. The first is that an individual's educational entitlement in a system of lifelong education could consist of a mixture of compulsory schooling during the childhood years and voluntary participation beyond a certain age. However, in order to try and guarantee equal levels of public support for different people, a fixed entitlement to education (stated in the form of cost of the services to be provided) could be specified. This entitlement could then be taken up in different ways by different people. A second type of mixed financing could be achieved by making provision for payment of the cost of lifelong education partly from public funds, partly from private. The most obvious form of private contribution would consist of fees paid by learners, presumably beyond some specified age level (prior to which all provision would be paid for with public funds), another would be financing by employers.

A relatively simple device for realising both these approaches would be a system of educational vouchers. This idea has been the subject of political debate both in the United States and Great Britain. It has been attacked as an essentially 'conservative' measure that would have the effect of promoting private education at the expense of the public system. The undoubted political ramifications of this sort of change in financing higher education reinforces our earlier comments about the difficulties of introducing radical innovations in existing educational structures.

The past decade has seen a number of externally imposed changes in the way higher education is financed. Not only have governments begun to limit or reduce the funds they devote to universities, but they have also moved to tie such funds to specific strategic and programme objectives. These trends have been summarised by Scott (1985) who refers (p. 195) to a 'radical modification of the traditional relationship between higher education and society'. Scott believes that politicians, and to some extent the public, have become suspicious of the traditional autonomy universities have enjoyed, and that increasingly 'society will no longer accept higher education's own agenda for change, but will seek to impose its own' (p. 203).

One manifestation of this development is the increasing call for accountability by universities and for detailed scrutiny of activities or 'performance'. In some states of the USA, for example, funding has been directly tied to demonstration of learning gains on the part of students (the notion of 'value-added' education). Hence 'assessment' has come to be seen not just as a way of evaluating students, but as a means of appraising higher education itself (Blumenstyk and Magner, 1990). In Britain and Australia the notion of 'performance indicators' has become fashionable, and governments have said that they will make funding conditional on demonstrated achievement in both research and teaching (Cave, Hanney, and Kogan, 1991; Johnes and Taylor, 1990). In 1990 the British Committee of Vice-Chancellors and Principals set up an Academic Audit Unit for universities to review the ways that institutions were monitoring their teaching function and to recommend good practice. Insofar as they encourage attention to teaching and learning, such developments seem hopeful. Whether or not they will lead to increased emphasis on lifelong learning, as opposed to traditional teaching goals, depends on the way assessment and performance assessment are implemented. Clearly, proponents of lifelong education must be aware of the ideological implications of change, and not simply rely naively on public goodwill to effect a transformation of traditional practices.

Planning problems

Implementation of lifelong education would naturally raise special issues in the area of planning (see Schiefelbein, 1980). Existing methods of ascertaining which elements of the total system need to be expanded might well be no longer effective. Little is known, for instance, about participation rates in lifelong education (except that they are, as yet, disappointingly low), about the reaction of employers to further learning, about effects of learning upon motivation for more and about payoffs of lifelong learning in the form of career benefits. Another related issue concerns the demand for education at various ages and in various forms. The key questions here would have to be identified, and appropriate methods for obtaining the necessary data developed. For instance, it is possible that there would be initially an enormous growth in the demand for educational services, but, as the overall level of education in a society rose, the demand might fall off. This would be expected to occur if, among other things, the benefits resulting from increases in knowledge grew to be less significant. (It could also occur if self-directed learning became a norm, a result that would be favourably regarded by most proponents of lifelong education.) Further possible problems include conflicts between different ways of delivering education, or over priorities for different learner groups. Planners would be called upon to give advice about which learners should be most strongly supported – for instance, those with the least prior education, those with the most (since they have already proved their ability to benefit from learning experiences) and those with the largest amount of unrealised potential – and what forms of investment would yield the greatest benefits to society.

The danger of bureaucracy

The organised support of lifelong learning by means of a system of lifelong education is fraught with difficulties. The most fundamental of these is the fact that, as Walker (1980) pointed out, the idea of deliberately setting out to bureaucratise an innovation is in itself 'inherently obnoxious'. Put slightly differently, bureaucracies as we have come to know them are not usually regarded as ideal bodies for promoting change. There seems to be a contradiction between the call for innovative and flexible forms of education and the belief that this can be achieved through a system or organisation, especially where the educational system concerned is to be both lifelong and also 'lifewide' (covering all settings in which people learn). There seems therefore, to be an irreconcilable contradiction between the desire to foster lifelong learning as an instrument of emancipation and the actual provision of organised educational services capable of achieving this goal. It is obvious, nonetheless, that some degree of organisation of lifelong education is unavoidable, and that its proponents will have to learn to live with this apparent paradox. At the same time it will be necessary to remain continually on guard against the danger that the machinery of lifelong education could become so cumbersome as to defeat its own purposes. In other words, it is important that the systematisation and organisation of lifelong learning should not translate into excessive control or rigidity (Pineau, 1980).

Moving towards lifelong education

It is apparent from the foregoing discussions that the actual implementation of the principles of lifelong education in institutions of higher education is beset by considerable difficulties. Indeed, an overnight wholesale change is hardly to be expected. More likely is a piecemeal implementation of certain elements of lifelong education over a long period of time – what Duke (1976) described as implementation by degrees. The question now arises of how to encourage moves in the right direction.

Criteria

While lifelong learning is unlikely to produce immediate and radical change in conventional systems of higher education, it makes sense to be on the alert for examples of partial shifts in philosophy and practice that go some way towards fulfilling our goals for this new approach. In Chapter 3 (e.g. Table 3.1), we have already referred to criteria that relate to personal development of learners and lifelong learning skills.

It is also possible to list criteria for organisational or institutional development. For example, such a list might include diversity and democratisation of institutions, debureaucratisation, increasing recognition of work and life experiences as educational and vocational credentials, moves towards integration of learning experiences in formal institutions with work and everyday life, and similar developments. Duke sees such changes as gaining impetus over the next 25 years.

Indicators

Gelpi (1980) has extended these criteria and has stated them in somewhat more concrete terms, suggesting a number of 'indicators' for ascertaining the extent to which lifelong education principles have penetrated a functioning system. These indicators could help in developing methods for evaluating existing institutions according to the principles of lifelong education. Different indicators may be more difficult to implement in some countries than in others, while some indicators may be more or less significant in particular societies, according to the objectives of the country in question. Among the indicators Gelpi mentioned are:

- participation of workers' children in all levels of education;
- participation of workers themselves in all levels;
- use in the formal system of instructors who are not professional teachers;
- active participation of workers as educational personnel;
- decompartmentalisation of the different streams of education;
- introduction of folk culture as an integral part of formal curriculum;
- integration of general and vocational education;
- incorporation of work experience into the formal educational process;
- participation of students in the management of educational institutions;
- significant development of self-instructional procedures and of research in this area;
- provision of appropriate facilities (paid leave, suitable learning materials, etc.) to groups with special needs, in order to enable them to profit from the educational system.

It is important that these indicators be looked at in a qualitative as well as a quantitative way. In other words, it is not simply a matter of, let us say, increasing the number of workers' children participating in a particular sector of the system, but of specifying the kind of participation and the results to which it leads, as described in our earlier discussion of values in lifelong education.

Recapitulation

Attempts to implement the principles of lifelong education in institutions of higher education are confronted by formidable difficulties. These include the fact that organisations are inherently passive, that they tend towards institutionalisation and ritualism, that the purposes and support of higher education are basically conservative, that socialisation of higher education staff is extensive and effective, that academic professionals are given great latitude in their work activities, and that the processes of governance in higher education can often be an obstacle to change. Nonetheless, although educational change leading to the promotion of lifelong learning is difficult to implement, it is far from impossible. Indeed, while a good deal has been written about resistance to change, there is also much information about effective strategies for implementing innovation. In Chapter 5 we review some of the approaches that have been tried, and we examine the extent to which they have succeeded in introducing elements of lifelong education.

5 Lifelong learning and instructional methods: some promising approaches

In the previous two chapters we have argued for a system of higher education that would differ in many important respects from what is to be found in most traditional universities and colleges. These differences are philosophical, organisational and pedagogical. It is the latter that are the primary focus of this chapter, which is concerned with instructional methods conducive to the promotion of lifelong learning prerequisites and skills. A number of relevant themes have already been anticipated. For example, elsewhere we have stressed the importance of moving away from didactic, largely teacher-directed instruction towards approaches that stress active student involvement in and direction of their own learning. We have called for closer links between classroom instruction and the outside world, especially the world of work. We have drawn attention to the great importance of examination and assessment procedures in guiding learning activities, and the consequent need for evaluation techniques that test relevant characteristics in an appropriate manner. In particular, we have pointed out that lifelong learning skills are likely to involve sophisticated processes of decision making and problem solving, as opposed to simply the memorisation of facts. This should be reflected in the way learning is tested, whether such appraisal is intended to provide information to students or to yield some credential for external use. Yet another theme in previous chapters has been the importance of integrating concepts from a variety of disciplines. Finally, we have stressed the very diverse characteristics of potential lifelong learners – diverse in terms of their age, background and experience, attitudes, and approaches to learning.

If instruction is to promote lifelong learning among this very heterogeneous group, there will be a need to employ instructional strategies that differ substantially from those used in many traditional colleges and universities. The present chapter reviews some of the strategies that have been successfully adopted in higher education to promote the types of learning we regard as desirable for an effective system of lifelong education. The developments reviewed here embrace teaching and learning methods, as well as means for 'delivering' instruction in ways that make learning opportunities far more accessible in terms of times, places and types of learners.

Distance learning

A major barrier for many potential students in higher education is the physical constraint imposed by the times and locations at which courses are provided. Unlike schools, in most countries institutions of post-secondary education are distributed fairly sparsely, and may not even be in the major centres of population (as in the case of some major state universities in the USA). In many instances, too, courses are offered primarily during the 'normal' working day (between the hours of 9 a.m. and 5 p.m.), on weekdays only, and for only part of the year. In the past this has been on the whole convenient for institutional staff as well as for a population of students who wish to attend classes during the 'working day', to study in the evenings and on weekends, and perhaps to take a paid job during the long summer vacation. Such arrangements are much less convenient for the growing populations of non-traditional students, described in Chapter 3, who must combine higher education with other responsibilities, which might embrace a 'full-time' career, and family responsibilities. One response to this need for more flexibility in provision of courses has been the growth of distance education.

Although the term 'distance education' is relatively new, the underlying concept has a long history, especially in primary and secondary education, where 'correspondence courses' have been offered for many years, especially in countries where the population is geographically scattered – such as Australia and Canada. The notion of providing instruction to students physically remote from the teacher and educational institution was undoubtedly born of necessity. This necessity can, however, be translated into a virtue by providing recognition of the fact that a great deal of learning, even in conventional educational settings, takes place in the absence of a teacher. For example, although the typical three weekly hours of lectures may be seen as equivalent to 'the course', student learning is by no means confined to activities in the lectures, but also encompasses reading the text and other relevant literature, work on essays and preparation for exams, discussions with other students and the whole process of reflecting upon the material from these sources. Clearly, for most students time spent in this type of learning activity is much greater than that spent attending lectures. Furthermore, a good deal of the learning in question (though not all) can be done without direct help from the teacher or educational establishment.

Models of distance learning in higher education

Smith and Stroud (1982) have reviewed different approaches to provision of distance learning opportunities in higher education in various parts of the world. A major distinction here is between programmes or courses offered under the auspices of an otherwise traditional institution and those provided by special-purpose colleges or universities that exist solely or primarily to cater for remote learners. In the first category are such operations as the University of Waterloo's correspondence programme, the off-campus programmes of Deakin University, Australia and the external courses of the University of the South Pacific that are offered via satellite to students scattered over the vast geographical area of the South Pacific islands.

While most institutions begin by offering traditional (on-campus) instruction and later may go on to develop distance learning courses, at Deakin University the process was reversed. The university was established in the first instance to provide distance education, and when it later began to enrol students into on-campus courses it was decided to make use of the materials that had already been prepared for remote learners, rather than having lecturers structure each course anew. Supplementary lectures and tutorials are provided for students who attend the university, but it remains true that the teaching of internal students is based on a system and approach developed for external students.

The most notable example of a special-purpose institution is the British Open University, while other models include consortia of institutions, such as the University of Mid-America. A similar cooperative effort involves the plans to use the European Space Agency's Olympus satellite to relay educational television programmes for adults, using specially reserved air time. Projects include a bilingual video magazine programme for enhancing language skills, exchange of patient information among psychiatric hospitals and transmission of multi-media packages for use by industrial trainers.

While early versions of distance teaching relied on print media distributed by post, there has been an increasing use of alternative communications technologies, in an attempt to make contact between teacher and learner more flexible and immediate. In particular, the rapid growth of information technology during the past two decades has led to considerable exploration of new approaches to communication as applied to distance instruction. Among the current innovations that have been tried, according to Smith and Stroud (1982), are:

- cable television;
- satellite transmission;
- Instructional Television Fixed Services (television transmission by microwave within a limited geographical area);
- Subsidiary Communication Multiplex Operation (which transmits information over the spare bandwidth on standard FM radio);
- slowscan television (by means of which pictures and graphics can be transmitted via telephone lines);
- videotex and teletext;
- 'electronic blackboards' (the image from a touch-sensitive blackboard is relayed via telephone lines to a television in a remote location);
- videocassettes and videodiscs;
- computer networks or linked microprocessors;
- 'teleconferencing' via a number of the media already mentioned (students 'meet' electronically at a particular time and can interact with the instructor and other students by means of an audio, and sometimes video, link).

Despite this plethora of new technologies, it is probably true to say that a good deal of distance instruction continues to rely heavily upon more old-fashioned media, such as print or audiocassettes.

External degrees

Although it is often thought that distance education is a new phenomenon that requires sophisticated technology, in fact the basic idea of receiving higher education without actually attending a university goes back at least 150 years to the foundation of the London University system of external qualifications. The basis of London's external degree system is remarkably simple. In contrast to more recent approaches to open education, the University does not involve itself with teaching, but instead is set up primarily as an examining body. Students must register for an external degree, must meet minimum entrance qualifications, pay fees and study for a minimum period of time – usually five years. However, how they prepare for degree examinations is left entirely up to each student. In fact, many elect to take formal courses related to the particular degree programme. These might be correspondence courses offered by commercial concerns or part-time evening courses taught by a variety of public and private institutions. In addition, a number of vacation courses are offered both by London and other universities. It is estimated that around 20 per cent of external students take no organised courses, but direct their own studies.

Sassoon (1982), the Secretary for External Students at London University, criticised a report by the British Advisory Council for Adult and Continuing Education which reviews policies and practices in British continuing education and part-time study. He made the point that the Council appears to equate studying with being enroled in a formal course, and he expressed concern that private study remains unrecognised as a method of education, implying that education is something that involves deliberate teaching, while what students acquire on their own initiative does not count.

'Open' learning systems

The term 'open learning' has recently become very fashionable in educational circles, although the definition of the expression is not entirely clear. In some instances 'open' appears to refer to the system for admitting students, and in other cases to the fact that instruction is widely disseminated over a large geographical area. Certainly most systems that describe themselves as involved in open learning provide teaching at a distance. A good review of open university systems in five different countries is provided by Vanderhayden and Brunel (1977). The institutions described include the Open University of Great Britain, Télé-Université of Quebec, the University Without Walls (USA), TIU of Sweden, and the Politechnika Telwizyjna, Poland. Nearly all the systems make use of television or radio, but they appear to reflect the character of their respective societies and the stage of cultural and technical evolution in each country.

The most famous institution of this sort is the British Open University (OU), which began as 'The University of the Air' but in fact teaches by a wide variety of different media, and provides an ambitious integrated and systematic approach to instruction. The media concerned include:

- written study guides or modules;
- television programmes;
- radio programmes and audio cassettes;
- published books;
- specially manufactured apparatus for certain scientific courses;
- personal contact with the instructor in charge of the course and with regional tutors and counsellors;
- telephone links with tutors and sometimes with other students;
- the opportunity to attend residential summer courses.

The OU uses a credit system (in contrast to most other British universities), registers some 70,000 students a year, and has so far granted over 100,000 degrees, including several hundred postgraduate degrees. A key element in its work is the course team, which develops instructional materials within disciplines, and coordinates the teaching elements that go together to make a course unit. Teams comprise academic staff, who write the basic material, television and radio producers, and an educational technologist who draws up course objectives and sees that they are logically related to the teaching material and methods employed. Developing a course this way takes at least two years, with a course life of four or five years (Knapper, 1980).

The Open University has spawned many imitations in other countries. For example, there is an open university in Germany and another in British Columbia, while Athabasca University in Alberta operates on similar lines. In some cases the British OU material has been used or adapted. In the People's Republic of China a TV university was founded in 1979, and in its first three years already graduated in excess of 78,000 students (Marshall, 1982). Japan opened a university of the air in 1984. The institution, which was in the planning stage for 14 years, had an initial quota of 10,000 students and intended to accommodate as many as half a million eventually, though early enrolments did not in fact meet expectations. It is planned that by 1996 the university will be able to reach 80 per cent of the Japanese population via satellite.

Bachelor's degrees (initially in the humanities and social sciences, but eventually in technical areas too) are awarded for the completion of 124 credits, taking at least four years, and the university is largely staffed by visiting academics from other Japanese institutions (Guild, 1982; O'Leary, 1982).

While most initiatives in open learning have been at the university level, the success of the Open University in Britain prompted the government to found an Open College and an 'Open Tech' to train technicians and supervisors, while an Open College of Advanced Education was established in South Australia in the early 1980s. Meanwhile the British Open University has created a continuing education programme which has developed a wide range of distance courses for business and industry and has proved very successful, from both an educational and financial standpoint. The programme offers mainly short courses and 'packs' for training, development, and updating of managers, scientists, and engineers in business and industry, and those working in the education, health and welfare professions. Courses are taught using structured distance learning materials, mainly print and audio or video cassettes, supplemented in many cases with live tuition and assessment through assignments and examinations. Packs can also be used for group study in the workplace or as part of in-house training activities. In 1987 more than 100 courses were available in this format, with some 18,000 students enroled and more than 73,000 packs sold. On a more pessimistic note, not all attempts to establish open learning systems have been successful. For example, the University of Mid-America consortium (referred to earlier), which was established in 1974 to develop radio and television courses, was forced to close down most of its operations in September 1982 due to lack of funds.

Psychological aspects of distance learning

Cropley and Kahl (1983) carried out a systematic comparison of distance and face-to-face learning in terms of the psychological factors involved. They argue that the difference between the two modes of learning is not *qualitative* but *quantitative*. In other words, features such as self-direction, internal motivation and learning in the absence of the teacher are not the exclusive preserve of one form of education, but are present in both to different degrees. This led the authors to suggest that conventional learning could be improved by giving greater emphasis to certain elements of distance education (self-direction, etc.) which are usually less common in face-to-face teaching, despite the fact that they are usually regarded as highly desirable. To push the argument a little further, it might be true that in some cases the physical presence of a teacher could actually *discourage* students from being more self-directed.

On the basis of their analysis Cropley and Kahl came to the conclusion that what they called the 'psychodynamics' (p. 36) of learning are somewhat different in distance students. They are required to take much more responsibility for their own learning than face-to-face learners, they must be self-starters who are capable of initiating and seeing through a learning activity without the direct supervision of a teacher, they must be able to work without direct feedback and without external rewards (such as an encouraging word from a teacher), and they must ignore distractions (since they mostly work at home in an environment which was designed for family life, not for the promotion of formal learning). These properties are also valuable in face-to-face learning, the difference being that in distance education they are absolutely necessary. The psychodynamic properties of distance learning just listed closely resemble the prerequisites for lifelong learning or the properties of the lifelong learner outlined in Chapter 3. Thus it seems, at least in principle, that distance education programmes have a great potential for the promotion of lifelong learning. In fact, however, much distance education may try to minimise student autonomy in planning and guiding their own study. Indeed many 'packaged' distance courses tend to be extremely prescriptive, perhaps out of a conviction that conventional forms of learning are the best, and that less traditional teaching/learning strategies are second rate or, as Knapper (1988b, p. 63) writes, 'back door' forms of higher education.

Knapper gives further examples of the way in which distance educators often strive to replicate face-to-face instruction to the maximum degree possible: by insisting that the same syllabus and examinations be used as in the on-campus version of the course, using a standard textbook, and sending out packages of highly structured lecture notes derived from the 'live' class. This is done in the interests of maintaining common standards between distance courses and those given in the more traditional manner. In doing this, however, distance educators may sacrifice the opportunity of challenging students to take more responsibility for their own learning instead of just relying on the authority of teacher and textbook writer.

The set of prerequisites for lifelong learning presented in Chapter 3 can be applied to the special case of distance education, and Knapper (1988b) reviews a number of distance teaching universities in terms of these criteria. He identifies a tendency for such institutions to move towards more traditional teaching approaches and suggests this is mainly because faculty are more familiar with didactic, teacher-centred approaches, having themselves been educated in this manner. Despite the growth of distance education worldwide, there are still very few programmes for training teachers in appropriate pedagogical strategies. And, for obvious logistical reasons, it is very difficult to involve distance students in course and curriculum planning, as recommended by advocates of lifelong learning.

Resistance from students also plays an important role. They may be overly respectful of established wisdom, or sceptical about the worth of learning other than in highly conventional settings. They may also be afraid of taking more responsibility for their own learning, doubtful about their own ability to plan and guide it, lacking in necessary knowledge and skills, or simply too comfortable with the passivity and dependency often fostered by conventional teaching and learning.

Linking education and work

Brzustowski (1983) has discussed a number of challenges to universities brought about by the changing nature of work, and the resulting need to forge much closer links between higher education and a wide range of work settings and employers. He points out that while the number of people who work with material goods is steadily declining, the number of workers who are involved in processing information in one form or another is increasing. Furthermore, in many societies people can expect to change jobs – and careers – much more frequently than in the past. This means that university graduates will have to acquire new knowledge on many occasions during their working lives. Brzustowski here is not referring simply to the continuing education function that has existed for many years in professions such as medicine. Instead he points to the need for retraining for different occupations or for radical role shifts within occupations. This might be accomplished by attending courses arranged by universities; on the other hand, much of the learning will necessarily have to be self-directed.

If changing skills and responsibilities are to be an increasing aspect of professional life (irrespective of cultural differences in the way such changes are made), then it is obviously essential to have the means for individuals to continue learning throughout their working lives and to forge links between educational institutions and the workplace. In the United States, the Massachusetts Institute of Technology in 1982 issued a report on engineering education that called for universities and industries to collaborate and take new initiatives in providing courses for the updating of engineers' skills and knowledge. The report draws attention to the point made elsewhere in this book that it is no longer possible to provide an adequate education in a concentrated dose of several years study at the start of an individual's career. To reach professional status, it is argued, requires a combination of academic learning and practical experience that needs to be continuously updated by both formal and informal study. The authors of the report refer to this as 'lifelong cooperative education', and call for the creation of a council, involving industry, professional societies and universities to help achieve this aim by preparing a national plan, raising the necessary funds and promoting new types of courses for the continuing education of engineers.

The report envisages a future situation in which off-campus teaching would be massively expanded to the point where there were ten times as many part-time students enroled in engineering as full-time students. To achieve this, the report recommends adoption on a national basis of a type of television teaching developed at Stanford University known as 'tutored video instruction'. In the Stanford system, recordings of engineering classes are shipped to various distant locations and played to small groups of students, assisted by a local tutor who is intended to facilitate discussion of issues raised on the tapes. (More complex questions are referred back to the lecturer by telephone and answers discussed at a subsequent tutorial.) Although the Stanford system does not appear particularly revolutionary from a pedagogical point of view, the MIT group feels that this sort of approach allows sufficient flexibility (e.g. in class scheduling) to form the basis of a national programme for lifelong cooperative engineering education, which they see as bringing to industry many of the attitudes and values of the academic world, and transferring industrial knowledge back to universities. Instead of the present sharp break between full-time study and full-time work, the report's authors see a gradual transition that would extend through most of an engineer's professional working life.

Important underlying premises of the report are the notion of jointly shared responsibility by both industries and universities for continuing professional education, the encouragement of formal study at the workplace both by employers and colleagues, and a collaboration between universities and industry to develop a means by which new knowledge can immediately be passed on to engineering practitioners. The report admits that bringing about such changes may be difficult because of the natural resistance of large organisations, whether academic or industrial: nonetheless the authors feel that the present rate of technological change requires drastic steps of the type they propose (Bruce, Siebert, Smullin, and Fano, 1982).

In Britain too there have been calls for closer links between higher education and industry, and one relevant initiative is the PICKUP programme (Professional, Industrial and Commercial Updating) sponsored by the government's Further Education Unit. One of its aims is to encourage new strategies for adult education, especially for those already in the workplace whose skills need updating (Garry and Cowan, 1986).

Two further examples of existing partnerships between industry and higher education are the National Technological University in the United States and the SATURN project in Europe. Both involve provision of distance education for the purpose of continuing professional education in the workplace, and both use the model of consortia involving higher education institutions (which generally provide the instruction) and industrial and commercial partners (who provide the students). In the case of SATURN, teaching is mainly by means of self-instructional course packages. At NTU instruction originates in member universities and is transmitted by satellite to receiving sites located on the premises of its industrial partners across North America. NTU was established in 1984, and by 1990 had 34 university members and 315 corporate receiving sites. It offers seven accredited Master's degree programs in Engineering and applied science.

Experiential education

In Chapter 4 we commented on the predominance of the lecture method in higher education, which we criticised as encouraging a passive approach to learning. A second feature of the lecture is that it generally involves a 'second-hand' condensation and interpretation of facts or ideas. This might under some circumstances be an advantage, but it is obviously inappropriate where a major goal of learning is to provide students with direct experience and the opportunity to learn through their own active involvement in a particular task. 'Learning by doing' has a long history in education. While it is often more difficult to set up and manage than more traditional, didactic instruction, potential benefits to learners are considerable. Of particular importance (and of a special relevance to lifelong education) is the capacity to facilitate transfer of learning skills to real-world situations. It is these characteristics of learning by doing and forging close links with the world of work that form the basis of 'experiential' education.

The term experiential education is relatively uncommon outside North America.* Although the adjective is not found in most dictionaries, the derivation of the word (from experience) is obvious enough. The origins of experiential education go back to the 1930s with the appearance of John Dewey's classic book, *Experience and Education* (Dewey, 1938). Since Dewey, the term has been used in a number of different ways; for example, some educators have used it to refer to the process of learning self-awareness, while in other instances experiential refers to learning 'on the job' or in some type of practical setting. Nonetheless, there are some common elements in the term as used within North American higher education. These include Dewey's notion of active learning (as opposed to passively listening to a lecture) and encouraging close links between learning and 'real life', especially work situations. Indeed, in the USA experiential learning has acquired the status of a 'movement', and there is an active Council for the Advancement of Experiential Learning (CAEL) which has several hundred institutional members and carries on a broad range of activities to fulfil the mandate implied by its title. There is also a British equivalent, the Learning from Experience Trust, which works with individuals, employers, and educational institutions to encourage and facilitate the assessment of prior learning through a programme of publications, research and consultancies, seminars and conferences.

While Dewey was concerned to bring real-life experiences into the conventional education system (as in the case of his famous laboratory school), for many American colleges experiential learning is equated with adult learning, and the experience referred to generally means experience in the world of work. Hence there is emphasis upon work/study programmes, and internships, including sandwich courses or

---

* In fact the term 'experiential training', in reference to professional education, appeared in the report of a British royal commission at least as long ago as 1970 (see Finniston, 1980).

cooperative education, which will be discussed at greater length in the following section. Much of the work of CAEL displays a considerable preoccupation with the 'credentialling' of prior work experience, and the organisation has developed complicated procedures for use by colleges and universities to assign appropriate credit hours for 'life experience'. This practice has been criticised on the grounds that it trivialises the purpose of higher education. For example, Sawhill (1978/79, p. 7) has asked, rhetorically, 'Can we name any human experience, no matter how recreational, private, or trivial, and be certain today that some institution of higher learning is not offering credit for it?' He goes on to argue that institutions have abused the system of awarding advanced standing to adults who have engaged in years of work or reading by 'their willingness to offer credit for experience that does not have a normal academic parallel'. Despite such criticisms, the practice of awarding academic credit for learning outside the formal education system appears to be growing. In Britain the Council for National Academic Awards has introduced a 'Credit Accumulation and Transfer Scheme' (CATS) with the aim of granting adult students credit for previous experience, both in formal study and in the workplace. Students can have their prior work evaluated by CNAA or by counsellors in various higher education institutions across the country. This counselling process also serves to guide students to appropriate courses and programmes in the formal education system. CATS now involves a large number of universities, polytechnics, and professional associations (Council for National Academic Awards, 1986; 1988).

A CAEL review of prevailing practices in experiential education (Davis and Knapp, 1978) showed that the predominant type of programme involved work in an off-campus setting, which could be under the formal sponsorship of an employer or agency, or could be unsponsored. Institutions included in the survey generally awarded credit for participation in the field setting, and this could be applied towards degree requirements. In a majority of cases this experiential learning was graded – indeed in some cases the educational institution charged a tuition fee related to the number of credits awarded. Assessment might be done by a supervisor at the placement or work site or by an instructor from the student's college or university. In any event, attempts were made to 'debrief' the students by means of a faculty interview once the outside work had been completed. Other characteristics of the programmes surveyed were the use of learning contracts and portfolios for assessment purposes. In Britain the Further

Education Unit (a division of the Department of Education and Science) has produced a guide to the assessment of experiential learning (Evans, 1987). It argues that higher education institutions should not only be ready to recognise 'knowledge and skills acquired through life and work experience', but also may need to consider changes in traditional curricula and teaching methods, so that what adult learners study in college 'builds on what they bring with them' (p.4). Such students may not be served best by 'off-the-shelf courses'.

CAEL and its member institutions have placed relatively less emphasis on experiential learning that involves 'traditional' students in the college classroom. Although there is a good deal of relevant activity both in the United States and elsewhere, it tends to be described by other terminology, such as 'self-directed learning', 'project-based instruction', and so on. We shall review relevant developments of this sort later in this chapter.

In some instances whole degree programmes have been created on the principle of experiential learning. One example is the Field Experience Program offered by the National College of Education in Lombard, Illinois – a private liberal arts institution. The programme offers a Bachelor of Arts degree in Applied Behavioral Sciences and is intended for adults who want to earn a qualification while maintaining their jobs, attending classes close to home that will fit in with their work schedules. Thus the programme stresses convenient class locations, recognition of experiential learning for credit and professionally relevant coursework. The curriculum calls for 42 four-hour weekly class sessions at a location agreed upon by the students concerned. Courses are taught in seminar/workshop format, and material focuses on organisational behaviour, supervision, interpersonal skills, management problems, etc.

In conjunction with this 'core curriculum', students design, implement and evaluate a research project related to their occupation or to their community. An important aim of the project work is to learn problem-solving techniques and research methodology, including statistical analysis and research report writing. Students are encouraged to form professional support groups drawing from their own personal, professional and technical backgrounds. There is also the possibility of earning credit for 'life learning', assessed on the basis of a relevant portfolio containing information about the student's previous college work, professional learning experiences, and so on. The portfolio is evaluated by college faculty to determine the amount of credit a student will be awarded in this way.

The Compact for Lifelong Educational Opportunities (CLEO) provides another example of an organisation whose rationale is the encouragement of experiential learning in higher education. CLEO is a consortium of colleges and universities in the Delaware Valley that acts as an information source and clearinghouse for potential adult students. Among the services provided are career information and self-administered career inventories, assessment of life-learning experiences for college credit, aptitude testing, and information on degree programmes, non-credit offerings, admissions criteria and locations of member institutions.

Practising the experiential education that it preaches, the National Society for Internships and Experiential Education, based in Washington, has used experiential learning approaches to foster exchange of information and resources for higher education professionals engaged in this field. The Peer Assistance Network (the full acronym is PANEL) offers a toll-free telephone advice service, referrals to other professions with relevant expertise in nearby locations, materials on topics in experiential education, and also encourages members to act as consultants to colleagues and to submit materials for distribution to other members.

The experiential learning movement has achieved such prominence in North America that efforts have been made to develop an underlying theoretical rationale derived from basic learning principles. The work of David Kolb is frequently used in this connection. His notion of the 'learning cycle' (see Kolb and Fry, 1975) involves a series of sequential steps that include:

- experiencing;
- publishing (sharing reactions and observations);
- processing (the systematic examination of commonly shared experience and identification of group dynamics);
- generalising (inferring principles about the real world);
- applying (planning more effective behaviour).

Experiential education as a 'movement' (for example, represented by CAEL and the Learning from Experience Trust) has so far been most successful in the United States and Britain. This may be in part because higher education institutions in many European nations have had an oversupply of traditional-age, full-time students, and have felt little pressure to become involved with the problematic idea of granting academic credit for 'life experiences'. This situation may change in response to new economic and social circumstances.

Sandwich courses and cooperative education

While experiential education is based on the notion of providing higher learning opportunities for those in the workforce, sandwich or cooperative education takes a somewhat different tack by, in essence, providing work experience for university students. Although in practice the two approaches may amount to the same thing, the underlying principles differ somewhat. Furthermore, whereas experiential education in North America has primarily involved adults in the workforce, most students in cooperative programmes have tended to be drawn from the traditional population of school leavers.

The latter is true both of the British sandwich courses and the North American coop programmes (referring to cooperation between education and industry). A typical programme involves a student in five or six work placements, each of four months duration, alternating with academic terms. Placements are generally made by the academic institution. The students are involved in productive work (for which they are paid at normal job rates), and their performance is supervised and evaluated both by the university and the employer. Academic requirements and coursework are the same as for non-cooperative study, but an additional equivalent amount of time is spent in the work situation. Since coop students generally work right through the year (instead of taking a long summer break), a complete coop programme typically lasts only a year or so longer than a traditional academic programme.

There are obvious advantages to the system both for the employer (who is provided with a year-round supply of students and can screen potential future employees) and for students (who have a source of income, chance of a job later and the opportunity to try out practical applications of the theoretical knowledge acquired in their academic studies). Perhaps the greatest benefits accrue to the institution which can use its physical and human resources more economically right through the year – although this generates some resistance from faculty who are used to a long summer vacation – and which can enrol more students without increasing physical facilities on campus. Indirect benefits include the impetus provided by students who are in frequent contact with the latest technology and current industrial processes: their experience provides a stimulus to members of faculty to remain abreast of current developments and the curriculum can thereby be made more relevant to the demands of the workplace. In addition, the close contacts between academia and industry are useful in themselves (as a way of encouraging a two-way exchange of ideas and information) and also carry prestige.

In several countries cooperative education programmes have proved extremely popular with the business community and with government – presumably because they are seen as encouraging pragmatic, career-related (but at the same time high quality) higher education, as opposed to the popular stereotype of the university as an ivory tower. The University of Waterloo, which was founded as a cooperative institution in 1957 with 75 engineering students, today has more than half of its 16,000 full-time students enroled in coop programmes, and makes placements in about 2,000 businesses and industries in various parts of Canada, as well as in other countries such as the USA, France, Germany, Australia and Japan. The university employs 36 coordinators to arrange suitable student placements and supervise the work experience. This type of activity makes for good public relations, and the institution has been singled out for praise by many leading industrialists and politicians. The idea has spread, and there are now more than 70 higher education institutions across Canada involved in cooperative education.

The discussion up to this point has described cooperative education in North America, primarily because of the large number of different types of coop programmes there and the rich documentation describing their organisation and activities. However, as mentioned earlier in this section, the British equivalent to cooperative education – sandwich courses – has a very long history. The oldest British course was established at Sunderland Technical College in 1903, and there were 43 such programmes in existence by 1974. Not surprisingly, sandwich courses blossomed within the polytechnic system although programmes have been under some constraint in the past few years because of a shortage of employment opportunities, especially for the young. On the whole, the British sandwich courses and North American coop programmes share a common philosophy, and are also alike in many organisational respects. The main differences (for example, the notion of industry-based programmes as opposed to the institution-based programmes that are almost universal in North America) are described by Grant (1971). As elsewhere in the world, British sandwich courses tend to be most common in engineering, but they also exist in business, architecture and, less commonly, in the humanities and social sciences.

Mosbacker (1975) reviewed cooperative education outside the United States and reported (p. 1) that 'in the last several years the growth has been so rapid that it is impossible to report an accurate count of institutions of higher learning offering such programs, although it is known the figure has topped the 900 mark'. There is an active international association for cooperative education which holds regular conferences every two years.

Other approaches

Cooperation with industry. Although cooperative education is by far the most common (and most documented) approach to providing students with appropriate work experience, there have been numerous other attempts to provide links between academic study and the needs and demands of business and industry. One example is McGill University's value engineering workshop, a project-based approach that involves students in an in-depth analysis of an industrial product or process with a view to improving its design. The workshop began in the university's Department of Mechanical Engineering in 1973, and is restricted to final-year students who work in teams of five with a company representative. The project teams work intensively over two or three weeks on an issue submitted by the company. So far the workshop has helped about 70 companies cut costs, while at the same time students involved have been able to apply academic and theoretical knowledge to practical industrial problems.

The companies pay a small fee to the university to cover organisational expenses, but it is estimated that to date savings of millions of dollars in production costs have resulted. For example, work for an aviation company on a costly fuel control system for aircraft turbine engines resulted in changes that could potentially save $135,000 over five years. Another project to improve performance of a scavenger pump for a diesel engine oil system resulted in a suggestion that the pump be completely eliminated and alternative changes be made to the design of the main oil pump instead. The potential savings here were a huge $1.2 million per annum (Breathnach, 1983). At the University of Waterloo the Department of Applied Mathematics for many years ran a 'problems clinic' in which small groups of senior undergraduate

111

students were assigned to work on industrial problems under faculty supervision. Clients included a steel works, a railway company and a bank, and the project was able to attract matching funds from the government of Ontario. A somewhat similar scheme was adopted in Britain by Leicester Polytechnic, which set up a limited company to undertake consultation on problems provided by local industry. Although much of the consultation was done by faculty, students were also brought into the process where appropriate (Jones, 1982).

An initiative that works in a somewhat different way involves personnel from industrial settings contributing to university teaching problems and, on occasion, curriculum design. This is sometimes accomplished through the mechanism of advisory bodies, such as the Waterloo Advisory Council. Schaffner (1982) has proposed organising teams of local industry personnel to teach one or more courses at a given institution – perhaps based on modules – during which appropriate individuals could handle different aspects such as theory, applications, design, and manufacturing. The course would be coordinated by the university engineering department. In fact an idea of this sort was put into practice for four years at the University of Illinois Institute of Technology for a senior undergraduate course on highway design, taught by employees of a local engineering consulting firm (Vey and Novick, 1974).

Northern Telecom, a large Canadian telecommunications manufacturer, devised an unusual but very tangible way of contributing to an academic teaching programme through its scheme for the fabrication of integrated circuits designed by students as part of their course requirements. The scheme arose because of the company's concern that industrial needs in their field were more advanced than anything universities could offer, and there was a lack of facilities within higher education institutions to test ideas experimentally (Breathnach, 1983).

Another potential, but generally disregarded, link between higher education institutions and employers is provided by graduates or, in American terms, *alumni*. Former students are already called upon to contribute funds by many North American institutions, and cooperative programmes frequently use *alumni* contacts to procure appropriate job placements. A further step might be to involve selected *alumni* in teaching – not by replicating the expertise of faculty, but by having them provide segments of instruction related to their own particular expertise in business or industry. This could have mutual benefits to higher education and employers, since the university could provide valuable help in updating the theoretical skills of industry personnel. Brzustowski (1983) talks about a relationship between former students and their university, using the metaphors of 'maintenance', 'check-up' and 'recall', reminiscent of the 'relationship between the purchaser of an automobile and its manufacturer' (p. 7).

Volunteer work. A somewhat different approach to linking universities and outside organisations is to make use of student experiences as volunteers (Greenberg, 1982). On many North American campuses outside agencies solicit student volunteers for work on a variety of projects relating to health, education and community development. For example, the University of Waterloo Psychology Department operated a volunteer programme for a number of years in which students were assigned to programmes related to their coursework in which for instance, students taking educational psychology might work in a school for retarded children. Reports were prepared on the experiences, and in some cases partial academic credit was awarded.

Another type of volunteer agency common on North American campuses are the Public Interest Research Groups (PIRGs) which are run and staffed by students and financially supported by student government. These groups, which were founded by Ralph Nader, have concerned themselves with a wide range of public issues (ranging from technology in the workplace to acid rain), and often perform both an educational and activist or lobbying role. The more successful groups have organised meetings, published newsletters and books, and their activities have involved students, academic staff and members of the general public. Although active participation is generally limited to a small proportion of the student body and the PIRGs have no official status within the institution's formal academic programme, in some cases the work of a group has had a direct influence upon a course or programme. For example, the Waterloo Public Interest Research Group sponsored a very successful symposium on the social impact of technology in 1981. This event attracted a wide range of academics and other members of the local community, and received considerable media attention. Proceedings of the symposium were published as a book (Elgie, 1982), and the following year a course on the same topic, taught by one of the original symposium participants, was introduced into the University's curriculum.

Some of the benefits of volunteer organisations are obvious: for example, the organisation receives a source of free assistance (and perhaps enthusiasm), while the student can learn a useful skill and also get the personal satisfaction of contributing time and effort to a worthwhile cause. It has also been suggested that volunteer organisations may be able to serve as 'educational brokers' between students and the real world. For example, Christopulos and Hafner (1982) describe the work of the American Heart Association and its attempts to serve as a broker between its own managers and higher education institutions, with the aim of providing relevant learner-centred graduate programmes.

Rosenman (1982) describes several partnerships between community-based organisations and colleges and universities to facilitate student experiential learning. For example, at Beacon College in Washington, D. C. students worked with outside advisers, drawn from local community groups, to help them design individualised degree curricula that reflected their own needs and concerns. The curriculum was essentially planned as a series of learning projects based on discussions between the external advisers, college staff and the students themselves. Learning methods frequently involved internships and applied projects in the local community, as well as more traditional tutorials, small group workshops and seminars. A common theme, however, is that all these activities draw heavily upon the learning resources in the students' own community.

In Britain the term 'study service' has been used to describe voluntary community activities undertaken by students as part of their academic programme (Goodlad, 1982). At least two types of learning are thought to accrue from the community service activity. In the first place, it is hoped that students will acquire information directly related to their academic courses. Secondly, it is expected that they will become more self-aware, learn to question their own attitudes, assumptions, and prejudices. Goodlad has reviewed this type of community service in various countries, and has commented that such volunteer work is by no means confined to the helping professions, but also exists in disciplines like law, management, engineering and the hard sciences – though, as expected, the volunteer work placements were primarily in government settings, especially social services departments.

Networking. An approach that also has the aim of forging links between university instructors, students and members of the local community is 'networking'. Sarason, Carroll, Maton, Cohen, and Lorentz (1977) have described the development of one such network (the 'Essex network'), which involves hundreds of people in several states in the USA and has mounted educational programmes that would otherwise have been impossible. Individuals from schools, colleges, universities, as well as from public and private agencies joined together to exchange resources on a 'barter-economy' basis for their mutual benefit. The authors claim that the Essex network demonstrates that there are ways of dealing with limited human resources to maximise community spirit, provide services and develop people's potential. While this sort of pooling of resources is relatively rare in higher education, the idea of the 'skills exchange' (in which members of the community offer their expertise in a wide variety of fields, either for payment or in exchange for someone else's expertise) has existed for some time in a number of Western cities, especially large North American centres such as Toronto and New York. With the rapid growth of electronic networks linked to microcomputers, it is possible that this type of activity may gain much greater currency in the years ahead.

Indeed a whole system for distributing software has grown up in North America based on electronic distribution of computer programs via networks such as PC-SIG. Authors submit their programs to the network, these are made available to members on an honour system; if the software is to the member's liking a fee is payable to the author. All this is done via 'electronic mail' (computers linked through the telephone network) and the concept is known as 'shareware'. Some of the networks embrace several continents, and members are encouraged to exchange their comments, make suggestions for improvements to software and provide general help to one another in using the system. Though certainly not 'higher education', such networks incorporate many of the principles of lifelong and lifewide learning.

Innovative approaches to teaching and learning

Individualised learning

A criticism of many traditional teaching methods is that they necessarily adopt a uniform approach to instruction in which all students receive the same information, regardless of their individual needs and characteristics. Yet for the system of lifelong and lifewide learning that we are advocating, the need to cater to individual student differences is crucial.

The term 'individualised learning' has been used for many years, and was initially developed out of dissatisfaction with traditional methods (such as the lecture), but without any particular relation to lifelong learning. Knapper (1980) reviewed different types of so-called individualised learning and pointed out that the extent to which such learning was truly 'individualised' varied greatly from one scheme to another. The degree to which individual differences are catered for is often quite small: for example, the programmed instruction developed for teaching machines in the 1950s was supposedly 'self-paced', but often this simply meant that students could work through the material at their preferred speed, while the actual content and order of presentation were exactly the same for all students. In this sense the degree of individualisation was no greater than would be possible in reading a book. Later versions of programmed instruction did attempt to structure the material in different ways for different students by 'branching', which made it possible for students who had mastered early parts of the programme to progress rapidly to more complex material, while students who were having difficulty could be routed through additional explanatory material that included a careful step-by-step explanation of particular points. In the case of computer-assisted instruction, the potential for this type of individualisation is considerable, although, as will be discussed in a later section on instructional technology, attempts at truly individualised CAI have been disappointing to date.

Two popular types of individualised learning that have had fairly widespread use in higher education are Keller's Personalised System of Instruction (PSI) and Postlethwait's Audio-Tutorial Method (see Knapper, 1980, for a fuller description of these approaches). Both these instructional methods involve a systematic approach to learning that includes specification of course objectives, the preparation of instructional 'modules' or self-contained units (which may be in written or oral form, depending on the approach adopted), and frequent testing of students for mastery of the different units. While these approaches appear to be successful in allowing students to master the material, they are individualised only in the sense that students work by themselves. Control of what is learned lies firmly in the hands of the instructor, and indeed assessment in most Keller Plan and Audio-Tutorial courses is confined to multiple-choice tests, so that the type of individualisation that might be encouraged by writing an essay or term paper is generally lacking.

Even with this limited way of catering to individual differences there are considerable logistical barriers to implementation, compared to teaching by the traditional lecture method. Learning spaces have to be organised in a different manner: for example, the Audio-Tutorial approach calls for specially equipped carrels, the room involved has to be available for many hours each day, and provision must be made for frequent testing and rapid feedback of results to students in the course. The different grading patterns produced by this sort of 'mastery learning' yield a distribution that does not resemble a normal curve, and this often causes administrative problems for department heads and registrars. Furthermore the course objectives often remain at a fairly basic level (knowledge and comprehension as opposed to analysis and synthesis). It is perhaps ironical that individualisation itself may be counterproductive in some ways, in the sense that students do not have the usual opportunity to collaborate and interact with their peers in the learning process (for this reason some courses of this type make a point of having students work in pairs on certain assignments). Finally, it might be argued that although this type of modular approach to teaching frequently seems to lead to more efficient learning of certain basic information and skills – possibly because it represents a more active approach than the lecture – on the other hand the highly organised method of presentation that is intrinsic to PSI and the Audio-Tutorial approach may perhaps give a misleading impression of how learning and problem solving take place in the real world.

For these reasons, many of the teaching methods that have been labelled as individualised instruction go only a small way towards fulfilling the aims we have set out for effective lifelong learning. Although they embody a certain degree of individualisation, they do not really enable students to tailor their learning experience to individual needs, nor do they make any attempt to provide different learning strategies based upon more fundamental individual differences, such as personality or study habits.

Independent learning projects

For several years the International Congress on Individualised Instruction (ICII) has promoted a variety of innovative teaching strategies (see Thomas, Habowsky, Doyle, and Hertzler, 1981). While some of these innovations embody the rather limited notions of individualisation referred to above, others incorporate a more sophisticated philosophy of individualised learning. For example, a leading figure in ICII has been Charles Wales, originator of Guided Design, which is an approach to problem solving that encourages a much greater degree of student initiative and freedom from instructor control than exists in either PSI or the Audio-Tutorial method.

True individualisation of instruction should facilitate lifelong learning by catering to different learner needs. Similarly, independent learning might be expected to fulfil the goal of encouraging students to direct their own learning and 'learn how to learn'. As in the case of individualised instruction, the concept of independent learning has been construed in different ways. To complicate matters further, a wide variety of different terms (including 'self-directed' learning and 'autonomous' learning) have been used to describe pedagogical approaches that we have here labelled 'independent' learning. In addition, approaches that stress student problem-solving ability, decision-making skills, and even creativity, frequently use teaching strategies that share a common aim of promoting effective self-directed or independent learning. The precise terminology employed is less important than the underlying learning processes involved. To take an example, Morgan (1983) discusses the theoretical aspects of project-based learning in higher education, but his comments and conclusions have broad applicability to the whole field of independent learning. Morgan's definition of project-based learning has two components: the first is a stress on students' responsibility for designing their own learning activities, and the second refers to active student involvement in the solution of a real-life problem as the best means of coming to understand the topic or issue.

Morgan distinguished three promising approaches to the use of independent learning projects in colleges and universities. The 'project exercise' involves a circumscribed project carried out as part of a traditional course, with topics generally specified by the instructor, and an assumption that the knowledge and techniques needed to complete the assignment will be those customarily used within the discipline and already familiar to students. Morgan's second model is the 'project component', where a project is not necessarily linked to an academic discipline, but is intended to fulfil broader, interdisciplinary aims, such as developing problem-solving skills and independent study. Here there is a stress on projects related to contemporary issues in the real world, and greater freedom of choice in choosing topics. The project component is not necessarily built upon knowledge and skills already acquired, and may indeed form part of a special purpose course outside the discipline-based curriculum. Morgan's third category of 'project orientation' refers to the use of project work as the basis for an entire curriculum or institution, with conventional didactic teaching provided only occasionally as supplementary instruction. Institutions organised along these lines include Roskilde and Aalborg in Denmark and the University of Bremen in West Germany.

The use in regular courses of small exercises closely tied to the methods and knowledge of a particular discipline (Morgan's 'model 1') is widespread in higher education. Indeed, there are considerable resemblances between this approach to project work and the traditional practicals or laboratories found in most science disciplines, which we have discussed in Chapter 4. Although use of projects in this way is a useful supplement to more passive types of learning, it is likely that more ambitious implementations of projects (as in Morgan's second and third models) will be needed to encourage effective problem-solving skills that could be transferred to real-world situations.

Guided design. One such approach is 'guided design', developed by Wales and Stager (1977), which is generally used in a way that Morgan would classify as 'project component'. The underlying philosophy of guided design is that effective problem solving or decision making is best learned by confronting a student with carefully designed but open-ended problems. Each problem is planned in such a way that, to arrive at a solution, students must make use of the discipline-based subject matter they are learning. At the same time, decision making and problem solving are seen as skills in their own right, and are taught explicitly, guided by printed materials prepared by the teacher that break down the problem-solving process and allow students to gain insight into their own intellectual approach to decision making. According to its originators, guided design is intended to be used where some type of professional training is involved that includes decision making as a central component, where there is an established body of information on which students can draw to help them make their decisions, and where the decisions made by professionals frequently have to be implemented by others. Hence the teaching of guided design actually models the approach of a professional working in the real world. For example, it emphasises learning from a wide variety of sources, working with open-ended problems and concentration on issues that are drawn from real life.

Students work in teams of five or six on problems formulated by the instructor. They must identify the 'real issue' and set goals for their work, as well as list underlying constraints, and facts; they are then required to generate possible solutions, choose a most likely solution, analyse and evaluate the solution, and report their results. A key feature of the approach is the provision of feedback to students at each step along the way. It is also emphasised that there is no one 'correct' solution and that the actual process of decision making and problem solving is more important than the particular solution arrived at. In fact, the guided design method requires students to examine closely the way in which they made their group decisions, and to try to learn from this experience and from the expertise of others in the team and in the class.

The amount of time devoted to a problem very much depends upon the nature of the problem itself and the background knowledge and experience of the students. Simple problems may take two or three hours, while more complex issues may occupy 15 hours of class time. While these activities are taking place, students are also expected to study an appropriate amount of subject matter outside the class, and to make use of this material as and when appropriate. Wales and Stager claim that learners not only acquire relevant knowledge in this way, but also develop an ability to learn independently, solve problems logically yet creatively, gather information from a variety of sources, make appropriate value judgements, work as part of a team and communicate their ideas to others.

Worksheets. A somewhat comparable approach to problem solving has been developed by Finkel and Monk (1978; 1979). They make use of a workshop format and 'worksheets', that can either comprise the basis of a course, or can be incorporated into a conventional teaching programme. The aim of the authors is to allow students to 'share the pleasures' of intellectual experience with instructors and with each other, in order to solve an open-ended problem included in the worksheet. Students work in teams that range in size from two to seven, and the teacher acts as a resource person – observing, giving guidance, asking questions and providing information in response to requests from particular groups or individuals. The rationale for this method of working is that students acquire cognitive skills by being directly engaged in intellectual activity, not merely by listening passively to lectures. The worksheet approach has been used in a variety of disciplines, and Finkel and Monk claim the experience has an effect not only on students' thinking abilities, but also on those of teachers: instructors who become involved in planning workshops and writing worksheets may have to 'rethink many fundamental questions in their field' (Finkel and Monk, 1979, p. 38). However, there is very little empirical research as yet that would provide scientific support for such conclusions.

The project orientation. Finding examples of 'project orientation' in higher education (where an entire curriculum or institution is built around the project approach) is obviously more difficult than for Morgan's two other components. Morgan himself (1983), however, cites instances of a number of European universities that were founded with an underlying educational philosophy that stressed the project approach. In addition, several of the experimental liberal arts colleges in the United States include project work as a major component of the curriculum: one example is Goddard College, which is described in more detail in the following chapter.

Another interesting implementation of the project orientation is the medical school at McMaster University in Hamilton, Ontario, which has served as the basis for a number of similar innovations in various parts of the world. The McMaster programme has the specific aim of producing self-directed learners who can recognise their own personal educational needs, select appropriate learning resources, and evaluate their own progress in studying (Ferrier, Marrin, and Seidman, 1988). The curriculum adopts an interdisciplinary problem-based approach in which students work in a sequence of small groups for three years. Students have to direct their own learning, and accept responsibility for the progress of the entire group in terms of objectives that are specified for the programme as a whole and for the individual segments. In each segment students work in a tutorial group of five plus a tutor, and the group must decide on the methods and strategies for learning to be employed. Groups are confronted with sets of problems, clinical experiences and a variety of additional resources. They are also encouraged to identify further problems, find other resources and even to specify new objectives. The goals for the various segments laid down by the programme administrators stress general skills and concepts rather than acquisition of facts. Final responsibility for evaluation rests with the tutor, but peer and self-evaluation form an additional important component.

Learning from peers

Earlier chapters have stressed the importance of learning from a variety of sources, and not relying upon the single authority of the teacher or textbook. Within educational institutions – as in the workplace and many other aspects of everyday life – colleagues can provide invaluable information and advice, yet learning from peers is often neglected, or even discouraged. In many of the attempts to implement lifelong learning, however, discussion with fellow students has been seen as an important component. For example, the McMaster problem-based curriculum, just discussed, emphasises peer learning at least as much as reliance on the instructional staff. As with project work, such learning can comprise merely one small component of a conventionally taught course, or can form the basis of an entire programme. Usually the term implies students working in groups on particular learning tasks, but other aspects of the approach include use of peers for student assessment and, in some cases, involvement of student groups in the actual planning of the course or curriculum.

A number of rationales have been given for encouraging students to learn from each other. At one extreme, peer learning has been seen primarily as a means of saving the instructor's time, especially in large classes, where the teacher or tutor may have only limited opportunities for contact with individual students. There is perhaps an implication here that learning from fellow students is inferior to learning from the teacher, but a good deal of research suggests tangible benefits of peer learning. Since a great deal of what a student learns in college takes place outside the classroom (over 70 per cent according to Wilson, 1966), then it seems likely that student colleagues will be a major influence.

Some commentators – such as Botkin, Elmandjra, and Malitza (1979) in an influential report for the Club of Rome – have gone so far as to argue that learning from fellow learners is essential in order to solve the awesome problems currently facing mankind. They see this as involving shared decision making, attitudes characterised by coopera-tion, dialogue and empathy, recognition of others' rights, and acceptance of a mutual obligation to tackle problems confronting society. If, as Botkin and his colleagues believe, decisions should be made communally and not left to an élite, then the importance of learning from and with others is clearly crucial. A similar point has been made by Schein (1972) in his report on professional education for the Carnegie Commission on Higher Education. He argued that the acute social, political, and economic problems facing contemporary society would require more than specialist knowledge from individual disciplines, and could only be tackled effectively by interdisciplinary teams who were trained to integrate knowledge and work together.

Peer learning has a long history in education, and many different terms have been used to describe the process, including 'cooperative learning' (not to be confused with the cooperative work/study programmes discussed earlier in this chapter), 'learning syndicates', 'learning cells', and 'study circles'. A more important distinction than nomenclature, however, involves the underlying objectives for peer learning.

In some instances students are used primarily as *counsellors* for their colleagues, as in Goldschmid's (1981) notion of 'parrainage'. Here advanced students volunteer to act as counsellors to first year students on a variety of issues, including study methods, exam preparation, etc. They are also encouraged to bring to the attention of the staff any learning problems that might be remedied by changes in the course organisation. The idea of providing encouragement and a structure to help each other in this way seems a useful step in enhancing study effectiveness, and has parallels with the notion of 'mentorship' in higher education – although the mentor in North American institutions is more usually assumed to be a staff member who serves as a role model and adviser (see Cook and Bonnett, 1981).

Another approach to peer learning has been to use students as *tutors* to their colleagues. In some instances this may simply mean better students serving as 'teaching assistants' for others in the class (for example, see Kabel, 1983). In other implementations the relationship between students is one of equality – for example, Goldschmid's (1971) idea of *learning dyads* or *learning cells*, in which small groups of students 'tutor' each other in turn in order to practise mastery of course material.

A more ambitious approach is the 'syndicate method' in which an entire course is organised on a group learning basis (Collier, 1983). In such a course the class is divided into groups (syndicates) of from four to eight students, and the main work of the class consists of assignments that are carried out on a cooperative basis by the teams. The teacher generally acts as a facilitator and resource person: students are encouraged to ask for consultation when necessary and also to seek out their own sources of information relating to the assignment.

Somewhat more controversial is the practice of involving students in *assessment procedures*. Heron (1981) has argued, however, that restricting assessment and grading to staff encourages extrinsic motivation for study and denies students the opportunity for fully autonomous learning. He points out, for example, that peer evaluation is the norm for academic staff in respect to their research work, where its effects on standards of excellence, critical enquiry, and personal development are often vigorously defended. Furthermore, peer and self-appraisal are common forms of assessment in the workplace. Heron goes on to elaborate a number of approaches to the involvement of students in their own assessment: these embrace different mixtures of self, peer and what he calls 'collaborative' assessment, in which the task is shared between instructor and students. Heron admits that having students rate themselves or colleagues requires a certain amount of affective and interpersonal sophistication, but argues that self and peer assessment can have important benefits for the process of learning as well as for mastery of content. He advocates a careful series of steps for those contemplating the use of peer assessment. These include deciding what to assess, which criteria to use in the assessment, how to apply these criteria and, lastly, actually carrying out the assessment. Boud (1986) provides a practical short guide to using student self-assessment in higher education.

Introducing such an approach to assessment and grading is likely to provoke some resistance from more traditionally minded colleagues – for example, on the grounds that students will not realistically assess their own work. A number of studies have examined marks assigned by peers and by a course instructor, and reported differences in assessment are remarkably few (see, for example, Boud and Falchikov, 1989; Orpen, 1982). Furthermore, it is possible for an instructor to involve students in the assessment process without necessarily abandoning final responsibility for assigning a mark in the course. Kabel (1983), for example, had students in his chemical engineering course suggest items for inclusion in the final examination: not only were many of the questions in fact used on the exam, but students could also receive additional credit for submitting particularly good items.

Such approaches are not without problems. For example, Collier (1983) points out that syndicate procedures often tend to result in less coverage of the syllabus – although the knowledge acquired in the course tends to be about the same. Even a strong advocate of small group teaching methods (Abercrombie, 1981) has cautioned about the difficulties of introducing these approaches, especially in a fairly conservative academic climate or where the instructors have little experience and training in how to facilitate group work. However, given the potential advantages of peer group techniques for enhancing lifelong learning skills, it seems worthwhile to encourage staff to acquire the necessary expertise so that such methods can be introduced with the maximum chance of success.

Alternative roles for teachers

Although our focus in this section has been primarily on the learner, the success of many of the innovations discussed above depends heavily upon the skill and enthusiasm of instructors in higher education, most of whom have had no formal training in pedagogy. Many critics of traditional learning methods have emphasised the importance of teachers in changing educational practice, and have suggested ways in which the role and duties of the instructor might be changed. For example, Goodlad, Pippard, and Bligh (1982) have proposed that instruction in universities might best be handled not by an individual teacher, but by course teams of three or four academic staff, as is done at the Open University. In this scheme, each team would have a 'course manager' who would supervise the preparation of courses, convene meetings of the team, prepare drafts of course material, monitor student performance and behaviour (including use of the library and other resources), be available to discuss study problems and obtain feedback from students on their experience in the course. The authors also suggest that the course manager should be familiar with the process of professional development and with aspects of student selection and assessment. In addition it is envisaged that the manager, working with other members of the course team, would help focus attention on the teaching process so that 'there would be an injection of educational knowledge into every working group' (p. 84). It is indeed this special responsibility for pedagogical matters that differentiates the proposed course manager from other types of ancillary teaching staff that have existed in some university systems for many years – such as the professional laboratory demonstrator.

Speaking in the context of lifelong education, Williams (1977) points out that many college and university teachers are probably poorly equipped to encourage appropriate learning skills, since few staff have any substantial experience of life outside education and 'particularly in higher education ... they may sometimes find their traditional authority eroded by having less knowledge than some of their students about the practical details and recent developments in areas in which they are theoretically expert' (p. 107). This suggests an approach to professional development that would involve closer links between universities and the workplace, an idea that has been discussed extensively in earlier sections. In the work/study programmes we have described the focus is primarily on providing relevant experience for *students*, yet teachers in such systems may have very few links with the outside work settings where the students are employed. An approach that focuses more on the needs of staff might involve exchanges of personnel between universities and business or industry. Sabbatical leave and secondments have always been regarded as a type of staff development, and some sabbaticals have been taken in commercial or industrial settings, especially by staff working in the business and technology fields.

A survey by the British Chemical Industry Training Board found considerable support for the idea of industry-university exchanges among heads of university and polytechnic departments of chemistry and chemical engineering, professional associations and senior industry officials. However, junior staff from both sectors were much less enthusiastic about the idea. Perhaps predictably, the academics believed that publication and research might suffer, while those from industry were dubious that academic experience would necessarily benefit their promotion prospects. The survey also revealed that where secondments had actually been arranged there had been difficulty in finding the most fruitful type of placement. For example, academics working in industry were automatically routed to the research or personnel departments, whereas those from industry inevitably wound up in the laboratory, and rarely had the opportunity to participate in administrative tasks or institutional decision making (*Times Higher Education Supplement* 1982). Clearly, even the availability of professional development opportunities does not mean that staff will always use them in ways that are most likely to transform basic practices and attitudes to the teaching task.

Innovative teaching and learning: some concluding comments

In this section we have only been able to touch upon a few of the many different instructional methods that seem to offer ways of encouraging lifelong learning. We have devoted most attention to project work, independent learning and peer group methods, firstly because they represent broad approaches that encompass many specific innovations, and secondly because these techniques appear to offer particular promise for our goal of promoting autonomous, self-directed learning.

Many interesting innovative methods have had to be omitted here. For example, the notion of learning contracts to facilitate independent study, the use of simulations and games in learning; the case study method developed in the Harvard School of Business and widely used in faculties of commerce and law, and the many techniques intended to promote creative problem solving. Indeed, our review of Huczynski's (1983) encyclopedic listing of instructional methods used in education and business reveals that no fewer than 76 entries describe techniques that could be said to facilitate lifelong learning. A random selection from these entries provides a diverse list of methods encompassing 'action learning', 'buzz groups', 'critical incident analysis', 'flexastudy', 'instrumental team learning', 'lateral thinking', 'mathetics', 'process analysis', 'self help groups', to mention just a small sample, in addition to numerous approaches that have been referred to specifically above. These techniques emphasise active student involvement in the learning task, use of group resources in learning, the importance of processing and reflecting on learning material instead of just 'receiving' it, bringing in a variety of learning resources to reflect or simulate real-life situations, and forcing creative approaches or solutions to problem solving and decision making.

The methods we have reviewed here (and many that we have not) carry with them a number of implications for the management of education and instruction. For example, they imply a change in the role of the teacher. In self-directed learning the instructor's primary responsibility is to give support and guidance, and help provide a framework for discovery and dialogue that will involve all members of the class – as opposed to merely telling students the right answers. A second, and related, consequence of most of these approaches is that the process of learning takes on more importance than the instructional content (Morgan, 1983).

Critics of such methods are likely to raise a number of arguments

(Cornwall, 1981), including the possibility that standards will fall because less information is assimilated. They will also suggest that it is faster and more efficient to use teacher-centred methods, especially where structured factual material is involved; that many students are unable or unwilling to take responsibility for their own learning; that independent learning causes difficulties in conducting objective assessment of students, and that the special expertise of instructors is not properly utilised when education places the major emphasis on students directing their own activities. All these criticisms contain a grain of truth, and those planning to adopt the various approaches outlined here would be wise to take account of such factors in planning their learning activities. In this regard, Heller, Reif, and Hungate (1983) provide some useful guidelines to teachers in higher education who wish to introduce self-directed problem-solving methods into their classrooms. These include the importance of making tacit processes explicit, encouraging students to talk openly about learning processes, providing carefully guided practice in problem solving, ensuring that students master the component procedures involved (through carefully structured exercises), emphasising both qualitative and quantitative thinking and designing evaluation procedures that really test understanding and thinking skills.

Recapitulation

This chapter has reviewed a variety of instructional methods that appear to show considerable promise for the encouragement of lifelong learning in higher education. We have explored three rather different themes. The first focused upon broadening the clientele in universities and colleges through distance learning. The second focus was upon programmes that attempt to forge links between higher education and the workplace. The third theme dealt with a variety of instructional methods that share an emphasis upon self-directed, independent learning leading to effective problem solving and decision making. Some of the ideas presented here have widespread currency, even in traditional educational circles. Others (such as student self-assessment) appear to be considerably more radical and controversial. It is important to note, however, that all the approaches discussed above have been applied successfully in one setting or another – although it does not follow that every innovation can be made to work in any context.

It is thus our contention that methods already exist that would encourage lifelong learning in colleges and universities. The next question is how the ideas discussed above might be implemented more widely, and this is the focus of Chapter 6.

6 Changing institutions to lifelong education

Chapter 5 reviewed a sample of the instructional approaches already used in higher education institutions that embody some of the principles of lifelong education. The examples of individualised instruction, project-based learning, distance education and attempts to forge links between the classroom and the workplace, represent only a few of the many instructional innovations that can be found in colleges and universities around the world. At the same time, it would be a mistake to believe that lifelong education is already being practised on a widespread basis (even if known by another name), or that post-secondary education is on the threshold of a transformation to instructional approaches that will indeed equip students with the competencies outlined earlier in this volume. On the contrary, despite these very promising trends it is necessary to repeat the dismal theme of earlier chapters: much teaching in higher education is of the traditional didactic sort, much learning is passive in nature, and the opportunities for horizontal and vertical integration of learning are limited.

This then raises the question of just how institutions of higher education might be transformed along the lines we are recommending, and this is the concern of the present chapter. The very fact that universities and colleges have used similar instructional methods for many years reinforces the likely difficulty of change, despite outside forces in society that make the need for new learning approaches increasingly urgent. Many studies of innovation, resistance to change and ways of surmounting this resistance have been carried out in higher education, and we shall describe some of this work below.

One approach to innovation is to bypass the traditional educational structures by founding entirely new institutions, and indeed some colleges have been set up with goals that include the fostering of self-directed learning skills. But there are also mechanisms within established colleges and universities that might be used to help transform teaching and learning practices. Such mechanisms include the work of instructional development units and study skills programmes, which have become widespread in many university and college systems during the past decade. Another development that has the potential to affect methods of teaching and learning in a profound way is information technology – in particular the use of computers to deliver instructional materials, relatively unrestricted by constraints of time and space. In the present chapter we examine some of these initiatives and consider the question of whether, and how, they may move instructional practice within higher education in a direction that is more in keeping with the principles of lifelong education outlined earlier.

Special-purpose institutions

As mentioned in Chapter 3, the past ten years have seen a marked increase in the number of non-traditional students entering higher education. There has also been a growth and/or expansion of new types of institutions, including polytechnics and community colleges, characterised by closer links between the teaching programmes and the outside world, including the workplace. Many of the new colleges have not been notable for radically new approaches to teaching and learning (*Times Higher Education Supplement*, 1983), partly because they have been staffed by people whose training and instructional role models are almost inevitably traditional. However, a distinguishing feature of polytechnics, community colleges, and similar institutions is that teaching duties do not on the whole have to conflict with scholarship and research, so that it might be thought that staff would be more open to changes in teaching methods, if only because instruction is their main responsibility. Indeed, staff development in college settings has often received considerable institutional support and acceptance by instructors (Greenaway and Mortimer, 1979). There is also research suggesting that most polytechnic students perceive their teaching to be better than university students do, show greater understanding and make better use of what they are taught – for example relying less on memorisation and regurgitating facts (Ramsden, 1983). This has been attributed in part to the influence of the Council for National Academic Awards, as well as to the work of educational development units, which have stimulated a much greater concern with course design and planning, teaching methods, and evaluation.

Other new institutions have been set up to cater (entirely or mainly) to students learning at a distance. We reviewed this type of establishment in our earlier discussion (in Chapter 5) of open learning systems – examples include the British Open University and its derivatives, Athabasca University, Deakin University, Massey University, the University of the South Pacific, and similar institutions. While few of these universities were established with the explicit purpose of fostering lifelong learning skills, they do fulfil some of the criteria for lifelong education outlined earlier.

In the first place they enable a much broader cross-section of the population to take advantage of higher education opportunities without the normal restrictions imposed by attendance at a conventional university. In addition, because distance education requires much more careful planning of instruction than is usually thought necessary in face-to-face teaching, many of the new open learning universities give a great deal of attention to the preparation of teaching materials. Furthermore, the resulting instructional process takes account of learner needs in a much more thoroughgoing way than is often seen in higher education, (for the simple reason that if it does not, the instruction is incomprehensible and students simply drop out of the programme – the usual supplementary support systems being just not available). Some of these institutions – the British Open University would be an example – have formalised this interest in teaching and learning methods to the extent of setting up advisory services for the academic staff on the preparation of course materials. In some cases too, the work of these agencies has demonstrated a concern with the principles of independent learning that are a major focus of interest of this book.

Still other institutions have been established specifically with the goal of fostering lifelong learning, although they may not have used this term. Some are relatively recent, and were founded during the time of great expansion (and radicalism) in the 1960s – for example, Roskilde University in Denmark. Roskilde's programmes place considerable emphasis on independent learning skills, project work and group interaction in student teams. A few institutions go back much further – for instance Goddard College in Vermont, whose curriculum is based on the principles of self-directed, independent, experiential 'learning by doing' as advocated by Dewey (1938). The aim is to produce students who are effective problem solvers in real-world settings.

Admission to the college is only partly based upon traditional high school transcripts and grade point averages; it also relies heavily on an autobiographical essay describing the students' educational motivations as well as a personal interview with college faculty. This emphasis upon oral and written communication is also an important component of the learning experience at Goddard. There is no set curriculum at the college, no fixed credit hours, very few lectures, and no formal examinations. Rather, the stress is on learning as an active, evolving process, which leads to students' gaining experience in a variety of practical projects. They may work in groups on a particular theme, but also help to formulate their own individual programme of study, which typically involves a good deal of independent work. Students must all complete a final major project that could involve an empirical research study, a photographic portfolio, even a novel. Although there are compulsory periods of residence in Plainfield, students may work away from the college, as long as they maintain contact with their adviser.

An extremely important element in Goddard's approach to education is evaluation, which is seen as an on-going formative activity that is an integral part of a student's learning experience. Learning processes are discussed explicitly, on the grounds that knowledge about educational development provides the student with a basis for self-criticism, self-insight and growth. At the end of each term students write a self-appraisal of what they have learned and how they have changed. The teacher also provides an evaluation of the unit or class concerned, and these appraisals are discussed between student and faculty member.

Great stress is placed upon involvement with the local community – for example the college runs a volunteer fire brigade and founded the local community health centre. Links between work and study are also stressed, even to the extent of having students carry out many of the manual tasks necessary to run the college, such as helping in the cafeteria or cleaning the premises. Students take an active role in college administration: for instance by their participation on the Goddard board.

Not surprisingly, Goddard College has not led an unruffled existence, and indeed it had to survive a major crisis that involved near bankruptcy and a threatened loss of accreditation. Such an intensive approach to lifelong learning goals is apparently difficult to sustain on a large scale. It has also proved difficult to find members of faculty who share the college's educational philosophy and have the qualities necessary to foster appropriate skills and attitudes in students. Nonetheless, to anticipate Chapter 7, it can be mentioned here that there is some empirical evidence of the college's success in fostering lifelong learning skills in its students. Certainly Goddard graduates are frequently successful after they leave the college: many go on to graduate school, and many succeed in the professions, especially in 'non-establishment' roles such as civil rights lawyers, environmental lobbyists, small business entrepreneurs, and similar occupations.

Another small liberal arts college that has tried to implement rather similar educational goals is Evergreen State College in Olympus, Washington. Publicly funded, Evergreen has a student enrolment of about 3,000, and its teaching programmes try to foster problem-solving skills, self-reliance, cooperation, communication and personal integrity through interdisciplinary seminars, which constitute the central mode of study. Other teaching approaches include internships and applied projects, and students are actively involved in assessing their own learning (Gray, 1990).

Goddard and Evergreen are unusual in that they have both survived and remained true to their original educational objectives. Other experimental colleges have not always been so fortunate. For example, in 1982, Evergreen sponsored a conference on experimental and alternative approaches to higher education that was attended by a wide variety of representatives from institutions across North America. A good many institutions had failed to survive, or their programmes had been modified to reflect a much more traditional concept of higher education. On the other hand, in many cases other institutions had sprung up to replace them. Furthermore, Bunting (1982), commenting on the Evergreen meeting, argues that the experimental colleges that have survived provide very important models for higher education, and may have a wider influence than the numbers of students enroled would suggest.

A much more informal approach to education than the ones discussed so far is exemplified by the 'free university' movement that sprang up in the USA in the early 1960s, and spread to many parts of the world. Free universities are organisations that offer informal courses to the general public, taught by citizens without particular academic qualifications other than a competence and interest in the topic they are teaching. The 'university' serves as a general (and very loose) organisational structure, but the individual courses are autonomous, with responsibility for content and methods resting with teachers and students. Some of these programmes are in fact sponsored by traditional universities, perhaps as part of the student government or continuing education activities. Others may be based on community organisations such as the YMCA or public library. Still other programmes are quite independent, perhaps organised by a few interested individuals, who serve in a voluntary capacity.

Free universities were initially set up on American college campuses as a reaction against traditional education. For example, they provided a forum to discuss and learn about social issues, and reflected a sense that education should be a community activity, and that students should have a major input into what, and how, they learn. Once the campus activism of the 1960s had died away, free universities began to take on a more community role as a way of providing an informal and inexpensive education for working adults. Classes typically take place in community centres, public libraries or private homes. Courses may include many topics, ranging from arts and crafts to more academic subjects. In Toronto, for example, the 'Skills Exchange' served as a clearinghouse for linking individuals with particular learning needs with others who wished to teach. A booklet listing a wide variety of courses (from philosophy to macramé) was widely distributed through-out the city free of charge; the Exchange offered no classroom facilities (classes generally took place in the instructor's home) but was responsible for disseminating information and monitoring the range of offerings. These administrative services were supported by levying a small additional charge that formed part of the course registration fee and was set in each case by the instructor concerned.

Free universities exemplify some of the principles of lifelong learning – for example that learning does not have to take place in special institutions, that learning from other people can be as important as learning from officially appointed teachers, and that learning pro-grammes should be self-directed. William Draves, national coordinator of the Free University Network (a national association of some 200 free universities in the United States) has described the guiding philosophy of the movement in terms of the principle that 'anyone can teach and anyone can learn' (Draves, 1981). At the same time, however, free universities may fail in some respects to meet the ideals of lifelong education, if only because they tend to attract students who already have a well developed interest in education: typically, job holders with a college education. Hence while such institutions may indeed provide opportunities for lifelong learning, they may do less to teach the appropriate skills to those who do not already possess them.

Somewhat similar in philosophy, but catering specifically to older learners (typically those over 60 years of age), are the 'Universities of the Third Age'. The idea for these institutions originated in the late 1970s in France, where there are such organisations in 60 cities. The movement has since spread throughout Europe, Asia, South and North America. The first similar enterprise in Britain was established in London in 1983, with some 400 students involved in self-directed study embracing subjects from French to psychology. Classes are non-credit, enrolment fees are extremely modest, and both staff and students are drawn from the ranks of the retired. Administrators and teachers provide their services free or for a token fee.

Although the Universities of the Third Age are completely controlled by the volunteer staff and students, the formal educational establishment has often been helpful in providing facilities: for example, the London institution holds classes at various university and polytechnic sites (Stevens, 1983). Thompson, Itzin and Abendstern (1990) outline some aspects of the Bath University of the Third Age, which has 350 members aged between 50 and 94. This institution is a cooperative and receives no state funding; it is not attached to a conventional university and does not draw its teachers from the ranks of traditional academics. The basic teaching unit is a 'study group' consisting of two or more people with a common interest. Although larger groups often appoint a coordinator, each student is expected to function as a member of a 'learning exchange' – for instance, by taking responsibility for the organisation of one group meeting, or perhaps by writing a paper which the whole group considers. Typical subjects studied include oral history, current affairs, music, European politics, photography and even gardening. In North America a very similar development has been the Elderhostel movement in which older adults use university campuses during the summer vacation for a type of 'learning holiday'. As with the free universities, the Universities of the Third Age tend to attract individuals with above average educational backgrounds, as opposed to people who have had fewer opportunities to study (Stevens, 1983).

While some institutions have operated outside the formal educational system (the free universities), and some have been received with benevolent tolerance by the educational establishment (for example, the Universities of the Third Age), others have provoked hostile reactions from their more conventional counterparts as a result of their incursions into non-traditional forms of higher education. One example is National University, founded in the USA in 1972 with the aim of providing higher education in a non-traditional manner for students (mainly middle managers and technicians) who could not attend a conventional institution with its inflexible admissions standards, tight class schedules and rigid academic calendars.

In 1977 National was an accredited university with 2,000 students enroled in more than a dozen degree programmes, primarily in the business and public administration areas. All students had at least five years of working experience, while faculty members were mainly part-timers from business and industry who taught two or three courses a year. The university offered simple admission and registration procedures, comfortable and convenient locations and class times, and generous credit for prior learning activities. However, it attracted considerable criticism from the Higher Education Association of San Diego, a consortium of 16 accredited colleges and universities, ostensibly on the basis of National's limited curriculum, the qualifications of its adjunct faculty and its admissions standards. In response, the university retorted that it was being singled out simply because it was non-traditional and successful (Watkins, 1977). In fact by 1983 National was operating five campuses across California and had an enrolment of over 10,000 students. It had retained its accredited status, and a doctoral programme was in the planning stage (Harper, 1983).

Certainly, any institution that is perceived as a direct rival to traditional colleges and universities is likely – for both good and bad reasons – to attract their attention and, on occasion, their criticism. The wide range of alternative higher education institutions (a small sample of which have been described here) is still very small in comparison to the higher education establishment. These alternative colleges may have profound effects upon enhancing lifelong learning skills in some individuals, but they are unlikely to bring about the transformation of higher education that might foster lifelong learning skills on a broad scale. At the same time, these experimental and innovative institutions often serve as an example and testing ground for ideas and practices that can later be incorporated into traditional institutions. Changing teaching and learning practices within the educational establishment is discussed in the remainder of this chapter.

Changing teaching and learning methods

Instructional development programmes

Although teaching constitutes the main raison d'être for most higher education institutions, there is the irony that few instructional staff ever receive formal training in methods of teaching and learning, and are appointed almost exclusively on the basis of their expertise within a discipline, as exemplified by research publications. When universities were relatively small, student-staff ratios low and only a few hours each week were devoted to formal lectures, there were relatively few complaints about the quality of teaching. The highly selected group of students who entered higher education prior to the 1950s was, for the most part, well-qualified and motivated; furthermore, most institutions and departments were small enough to allow considerable informal contact between staff and students, to the extent that any deficiencies in the lecture method were often masked. This situation changed rapidly and extensively during the period of great growth in the 1950s and 1960s. Not only were there vastly more students, much larger classes and increased staff work loads, but the types of students entering college and university were different in terms of attitudes, knowledge and approach to the learning task. Hence teaching methods that had served in the past came under increasing critical scrutiny, as higher education expanded and changed. The 1970s saw calls for institutions to be in some sense 'accountable', to demonstrate the value of university learning in terms of 'outside' criteria. This was linked to some criticism of prevailing teaching methods and – especially in North America – widespread use of student evaluations of instruction.

Between 1970 and 1975 over a thousand colleges and universities in the United States began some type of activity to help staff members improve their teaching (Centra, 1976), while similar developments took place in Canada, Britain and other Western European countries. In Australian universities a large number of teaching and learning units were established, many with substantial staff complements, and comparable activities were to be found even in some Third World institutions. In many cases these endeavours were fairly modest and were run on a voluntary basis – for example they might involve organisation of a series of seminars, or the appointment of senior staff members to act as 'mentors' to new instructors. In other institutions formal offices or units were established, ranging in size from one or two part-time staff to operations that employed 20 or more professionals, and encompassed such diverse activities as consultation on teaching, induction courses for new staff, automated test scoring services, audiovisual aids and graphics services.

By the mid 1970s these services (which we refer to here by the term 'staff development') had become sufficiently institutionalised to constitute a type of 'movement'. Although staff development can hardly be thought of as a discipline or profession – for example Colleges of Education do not generally give degrees in the subject – there are many indications that it has managed to establish itself within higher education in many parts of the world. The annual conferences on improving university teaching, sponsored by the University of Maryland, have been held in many parts of the world for almost 20 years and attract several hundred participants from dozens of different countries: a large number of those organising the conferences and presenting papers are professional staff developers. Other indicators include the existence of professional associations such as the:

- Professional and Organizational Development Network in the United States;
- European Association for Research and Development in Higher Education;
- Higher Education Research and Development Association of Australasia;
- Society for Teaching and Learning in Higher Education in Canada;

and journals devoted to the field (*Higher Education Research and Development, Journal of Staff, Program, and Organization Development*).

Teather (1979) has carried out an international review of staff development activities, covering a large number of programmes in over ten countries, ranging from the United States to India. The major activities described in the various chapters include provision of an information clearinghouse and resource collection, publication of a broad range of materials (from newsletters to specialised manuals), organisation of courses, workshops and seminars, consultation with individual teachers, administrators, committees and other groups, evaluation of teaching, conduct of research on teaching and learning, contributing to course planning and curriculum development, giving policy advice and establishment of small grants programmes intended to encourage instructional innovation. In addition to units within individual institutions, several countries have established national organisations to foster and support staff development activities, such as the Staff Training Unit of the Swedish National Board of Colleges and Universities.

Of particular interest from the point of view of lifelong education are Teather's chapters on the former German Democratic Republic (GDR) and Sweden. In the GDR a nationally organised training course in 'university pedagogics' included the aims of 'stimulating and helping the students to do creative academic work on their own initiative', 'guiding the students in the practical application of academic knowledge' and 'promoting the development of the student's personality' (Möhle, 1979, p. 133). The Swedish Staff Development Unit includes in its criteria for assessing competence in university teaching 'the ability to cooperate with the students and to arrange learning situations in which students' creativity and capacity for critical and constructive analysis is fostered' (Jalling, 1979, p. 208). Furthermore, one of the regularly offered national staff development courses run by the Swedish National Board includes a lengthy component on project-based instruction, which is contrasted with teacher-centred learning; practising what it preaches, this course has participating staff take on the role of students in different learning approaches.

Since, by definition, those involved in staff development have a commitment to the improvement of teaching, it is not surprising that many of them are concerned with the philosophy and implementation of lifelong education. Indeed some substantial contributions to the understanding of lifelong learning have come from staff developers (e.g. Boud, 1988; Lindquist, 1978a, 1978b, 1979). At the same time, political pressures within universities tend to deter instructional development units from urging fundamental change in university teaching and learning practice. Since units are often regarded as a 'fringe' activity, their staff rarely have the freedom to speak out frankly on fundamental issues without running the risk of considerable criticism from the teaching staff. There is also some evidence that those least inclined to participate in staff development activities are instructors who are in greatest need of improvement (Konrad, 1983). Furthermore, a good deal of instructional development activity may be devoted to 'tinkering' with the existing system – for instance giving workshops to improve the lecture method, giving advice on how to construct multiple-choice examinations. (Geis and Smith, 1983; Gustafson, 1977; Gustafson and Bratton, 1983). This may actually hinder the acquisition of lifelong learning skills, which often demands much more radical institutional reorganisation and a move away from teacher-dominated learning.

It would be reassuring in a sense to think that this inability to make fundamental changes in instructional methods lies at the root of the instructional development movement's failure to make the impact on university teaching and learning that some critics have hoped for. However, it seems more plausible that the slow rate of change has more to do with the general indifference of staff to the teaching function, and the general university ethos that stresses research more than teaching, among similar factors.

One of the most promising activities of instructional development units are their involvement in evaluation and in research on the learning process itself. Evaluation schemes have tended to focus primarily on student ratings of instruction, and many of the questions on rating forms relate to presentation techniques rather than opinions about the amount and type of learning that has taken place. In this sense, it is possible that evaluation reinforces traditional approaches to instruction (Wilson, 1987). On the other hand, data about how students respond to teaching is certainly better than no information (or data based on coffee room hearsay). Furthermore, summative evaluation schemes that influence administrative decisions about promotion, tenure, and so on, at least have the merit of reinforcing the importance of the teaching role. Many rating forms include at least some items that ask about the quality of learning, and more recent approaches to instructional evaluation (such as the teaching dossier – see Shore, Foster, Knapper, Nadeau, Neill, and Sim, 1986) have considerably enlarged the scope of the process from a reliance on student questionnaires to a more general concern with learning outcomes. Hence while teaching evaluation in its present form may not contribute significantly to achieving the goals of lifelong education, it can serve as a basis for scrutinising present teaching practices and appraising instructional changes that might encourage a more independent type of learning.

Research done by instructional development units may or may not have any relevance to the promotion of lifelong education. However, there resides in the units considerable expertise (perhaps the principal expertise available at the institution) in conducting investigations into educational practices within the university and their effects upon learning. Research of this type, done by instructional developers, has already gone some way towards revealing the shortcomings of traditional instruction (e.g. investigations of grading practices, studies of the effectiveness of the lecture, and so on, many of which are referred to in this book). It seems likely that in-house research of this type could provide an extremely useful basis for developing teaching and learning methods that might encourage practices consistent with the principles of lifelong education spelled out in earlier chapters.

Study skills programmes

Just as instructional development units have collaborated with teachers in higher education to effect change, there have also been efforts to work directly with students to improve their learning skills. Study skills programmes exist in many universities around the world and there are numerous textbooks on effective study techniques aimed at the university and college student. (Main, 1980, and Marshall and Rowland, 1981, provide relevant bibliographies.) In some cases study skills programmes are part of the instructional development office. A more usual model, however, is to offer the programme through the university counselling service.

These programmes have a great deal in common – they generally focus on improving reading skills, time management and effective organisation of study, notetaking and preparation for examinations. In addition they often offer instruction in effective writing, preparing essays and reports and similar skills. It might be thought that such activities are remedial (in the sense used in Chapter 1), but in fact they attract many good students, as well as weak ones. The fact that such programmes are popular with students – at least in North American universities – shows, if nothing else, how many of the demands placed upon students in the instructional situation are never made explicit in classes, thus forcing learners to seek the relevant information from outside sources.

Just as instructional development can be criticised on the grounds that it simply tinkers with existing (and, we would argue, largely inappropriate) teaching methods, so study skills workshops that focus on notetaking, examination preparation, and similar techniques could be said merely to equip students with ways of making the best of inappropriate instructional methods. On the whole, this is somewhat unfair to study skills advisers, since they are rarely in a position to change teaching practice within their institution, and have to respond to a reality in which students wish to perform well in the actual learning context that they encounter in higher education. Furthermore, some of the common components of study skills courses do deal with aptitudes that are perfectly consistent with lifelong learning – such as the ability to organise study, manage time, learn from peers, communicate with others and read and write reports.

One approach to study skills that encourages students to be independent learners and continually question their own learning processes is outlined in the handbook prepared by Marshall and Rowland (1981). Although the familiar topics of taking better lecture notes and preparing for examinations are covered in the text, the authors encourage a generally critical attitude about the general purpose of education and urge students to examine their expectations, choices and decisions. They are told how to seek guidance from their peers (as well as from academic staff), how to ask questions, even whether or why material encountered in academic courses is worth remembering. The sections on examinations and grading are also somewhat unusual in that they focus on how students may derive personal benefit from the evaluation process and use it to their own ends.

Study skills courses have also been criticised on other grounds. For example, it is argued that they are not fully integrated into the regular academic work of the student and are seen as rather gimmicky, 'quick fix' solutions to problems that require much more fundamental changes in attitudes and study habits. It is thus argued that techniques learned in a short course of a few hours will be difficult to transfer to the real learning situation that students encounter in a variety of classes, tasks and subject matters (see, for example, Gibbs, 1977; Raaheim and Wankowski, 1981).

Among the solutions that have been suggested are provision of closer links with the subject matter being studied in classes, and the elevation of study skills to a more prominent place in the curriculum, where they can receive more time and attention, attain a generally higher profile and greater credibility and, as a result, involve more students. This is the approach used in Murdoch University's 'trunk courses', which are required of all in-coming students and include a major component of study skills techniques. The trunk courses adopt a broadly-based interdisciplinary approach, and tutors are encouraged to introduce learning skills strategies as they teach the 'academic' content. In addition, a special segment of the course on appropriate learning skills is taught by tutors under the guidance of the University's study skills

143

adviser. Special tutorials are offered for particular types of learning problem, such as those involved in mathematical skills, and additional assistance is available on a voluntary basis (with students who take part being given dispensation from part of the course requirements). Every effort is made to encourage peer learning to supplement the understanding of study techniques learned in the more orthodox tutorials.

The Murdoch situation is clearly atypical, and in many institutions it may be difficult to integrate study skills techniques into regular discipline-based coursework, as has been suggested by Marshall, Gibbs and others. In many cases the teaching staff will have little interest in taking time to cover basic study techniques – or may lack the skills to do so effectively. However, despite the criticism of Gibbs, many study skills programmes do in fact try to relate the techniques they teach to the real academic problems faced by students – for example by having students bring to the study skills workshops problems and examples encountered in their normal courses.

Non-traditional students present a special challenge for study skills programmes: for example, foreign students, students from minority groups, and mature students all enter the special environment of higher education with backgrounds and aptitudes that may differ markedly from those of students who come from the traditional secondary school system. Since in many countries adult learners form an increasingly large segment of the student body, this group has been of special concern. Among the particular study problems identified are those of reentering the education system, coping with mathematics and science subjects, combining academic work with other commitments, and integrating life experiences with what is learned in the classroom. Many institutions have organised special study programmes for mature students, and a common element of such programmes is the use of peers to help with the learning task and provide a mutual support system (Knights and McDonald, 1982). Other strategies have included pre-enrolment of adult students to enable them to 'try out' university education before formally registering, linked with special counselling (McDonald and Knights, 1979).

The Swedish reform of higher education made provision for the admission of much greater numbers of mature students, and it is not surprising that the counselling needs and study habits of this group have been a special concern of educational researchers in that country. Abrahamsson (1976) reports on a project to investigate the way in which adult students were being integrated into Swedish universities.

The concerns of the investigation go well beyond the cosmetic approach of trying to equip these students with notetaking skills and giving them tips for examination preparation, and instead focus on how adults might be helped to cope with, among other considerations, role changes, individual lifecycle development, perception of reality, changing self-image and decision-making skills.

Whatever the shortcomings of study skills programmes, it seems clear that many students do need help with the process and practice of learning, and that students cannot be expected to magically acquire the techniques necessary for independent learning. This further implies a need to teach lifelong learning skills explicitly. Given the level of knowledge of rank and file faculty in such areas, it seems plausible that study skills advisers could have an important contribution to make in this area.

Instructional technology

At a time when there is widespread talk about an information revolution affecting the world as profoundly as the industrial revolution did 200 years ago, it is not surprising that information technology has been heralded as a force that will dramatically change the delivery and organisation of education, including higher education. Indeed the term 'revolution' has been used explicitly in the context of technology's potential effects on education. Ashby (Carnegie Foundation, 1972) sees information technology as a fourth revolution, following three previous revolutions that encompassed the establishment of the formal school, the transition of an education based upon speech to an education based on writing, and the invention of movable type and the printing press.

The term information technology is relatively new, but the older concept of educational technology has a history that goes back at least to the 1950s, and includes such innovations as programmed instruction, teaching machines and educational television. These developments did have at least a short term impact upon educational practice. For example, the programmed instruction movement in the 1950s received a great amount of attention in schools and universities, and caused many teachers to examine closely their educational objectives and instructional methods. Educational television, while its low level of acceptance within the traditional school and university proved a major disappointment to proponents of this new delivery system, has been used extensively in distance education (e.g. the Open University and its counterparts), although its relative importance here in relation to other more traditional media is probably much less than titles such as 'University of the Air' or 'Tél -Université' might imply.

Information technology links together the computer, with its immense capacity for storing and handling information, and electronic delivery systems that enable the information to be sent over great distances and to numerous reception points, virtually instantaneously. This new technology appears to have considerable implications for educational practice – not only in providing new ways of delivering learning materials (e.g. increasing access through distance learning), but also in affecting the ways in which instructional materials might be organised and presented.

Computer-based learning

There is nothing very new about the use of computers for instructional purposes. It was an obvious step in the early 1960s to develop versions of programmed instruction for use on a computer which was, even then, a more reliable delivery device than the old mechanical teaching machines. Computer-assisted instruction and its variants (computer-assisted learning, computer-based instruction, etc.), using large main-frame computers, were the subject of much development and experimentation during the 1960s and 1970s, especially in North America. Although experimentation with computer-assisted instruction continued in many colleges and universities, it would be true to say – as with so many of the innovations we have discussed – that the great majority of the work remained on an experimental level, while traditional teaching practices remained largely unchanged.

Computer-assisted instruction using large mainframe machines was frequently unwieldy and expensive. However, the advent of the microcomputer in the late 1970s seemed to offer a new opportunity for computer-based teaching to make a major contribution to educational practice. Nowadays micros are so cheap that most schools and many homes can afford to buy one; programmes on disc or tape can be produced cheaply and easily distributed; these factors in turn lead to greater incentives to individual teachers to write their own educational programmes. Technological advances have also meant that it is now possible to supplement the presentation of verbal information with graphics, audio, or even moving pictures (using videodisc). Hence it is not surprising that the microcomputer has more or less supplanted the mainframe as the preferred system for delivery of computer-based learning.

There is no doubt that the educational community – and the wider community of learners – have considerable expectations of the role that computers will play in education at all levels. Politicians responding to this pressure have initiated plans to equip schools with computing equipment, and in such countries as Canada and Britain microcomputers have been designed specifically for school use (see, for example, McLean, 1983).

How do these developments in information technology serve the need to equip students with lifelong learning skills? Two advantages often claimed for instructional technology are that it promotes active learning and provides a means of individualising learning. Both factors have been mentioned earlier as frequently lacking in traditional instruction, and hence a teaching method that would encourage such developments is of considerable interest to those wishing to promote more self-directed learning. In practice, the degree of active learner involvement and individualisation in computer-assisted instruction varies considerably from one situation to another. Computer-based educational programmes embrace several different instructional approaches. They may involve 'drill and practice' exercises (for example, in French grammar or arithmetic), 'tutorials', diagnosis and testing of student ability or learning, and simulations. The most common types of programmes are probably tutorials, in which the computer is used to present material, in much the same way as a textbook or lecturer, but with the added feature that comprehension or mastery is tested at regular intervals, with failure to answer the test question correctly often causing the learner to be routed to a remedial sequence of instruction.

The popularity of this type of computer-assisted instruction (or CAI) undoubtedly stems from the relative ease with which tutorial material can be written. Indeed, the various course-authoring languages (which enable educational programmes to be written without a sophisticated technical knowledge of computer programming) are nearly all based upon this approach to CAI. Programmes of this sort are very similar to most early programmed instruction. The 'activity' for the learner here is limited – indeed it is generally equivalent to the active learning involved in reading a textbook and answering questions embedded in the text. Individualisation can in principle be achieved to a quite considerable degree using complex branching sequences guided by sensitive diagnostic tests. In practice this potential advantage of the computer has rarely been fully exploited, and a good deal of the 'individualisation' that exists in computer-based learning programmes is no greater than was found in the much cruder, mechanical teaching machines of the 1950s.

In the case of drill and practice instruction, as the name suggests, the degree of active learning is usually considerable, and it is possible to tailor the learning material to the needs of the learner by presenting frequent examples of elements that the student is performing incorrectly and excluding material that has been mastered. Drill and practice programmes are usually at a fairly basic level, and are best suited to tasks where rote memorisation is required, or where experience is needed in applying certain basic principles such as grammatical rules. The fact that such applications are simple does not mean they are unimportant, and indeed a good deal of learning must be built upon these lower level skills. For the non-traditional student in particular, the advantage of being able to practise tasks of this sort by oneself and in one's own time seems obvious. Most drill and practice programmes to date have been prepared for students in the elementary and secondary school system, but there is no reason why they could not be developed for a wide range of applications related to higher education.

The use of computers to diagnose learner aptitudes, knowledge and even learning style seems to have considerable promise. Indeed, this was one of the earliest uses of computers in education, and is a feature of computer-managed instruction, in the course of which the machine administers tests and, on the basis of the results, routes individual students to appropriate (and not necessarily computer-based) instructional materials. Because of its considerable capacity for storing and manipulating data, the computer can, in principle, generate diagnostic questions from a large bank of items in order to pinpoint what students already know about a topic, and then provide appropriate guidance. Once again, this approach appears to have considerable potential for non-traditional students, who may have been out of the educational system for some years, but have acquired knowledge and skills from a variety of alternative sources.

Since independent and self-directed learning is an important aim of lifelong education, it would be valuable to have a tool that could be used to help guide students' learning activities, and do so in a much more rapid and precise manner than is normally possible through the more traditional means of discussions between teacher and learner. As always with computer-based systems, however, the machine is only as effective as the programme it has to work with. Developing diagnostic test banks and linking these to suggestions for study material is an extremely complex matter. It is even more difficult to go a step further and try to guide students on the basis of their study habits, preferred learning style, and similar factors. Hence the type of computer diagnosis we are describing here does not exist in the sophisticated format that would be desirable. Nonetheless, this seems an extremely fruitful area for future research and development.

An even more promising use of computer-based instruction involves simulation of some task or situation that would normally be difficult to bring into the classroom or home. The effectiveness of simulations to teach complicated skills has been known for some time – for example flight simulators used in pilot training. The computer is particularly suited to simulating a wide variety of situations, especially when linked to some device for presenting visual information, such as a videodisc player. Furthermore, simulations appear to be an inherently attractive form of learning because of their ability to engage the student in activity: indeed, simulation is a major element of computer games which constitute the main use of microcomputers among school-aged children. Numerous simulations have been devised for teaching in higher education. For example, the PLATO system simulates 'patients' who can present medical students with a variety of symptoms and respond to different intervention strategies or 'treatments'. There are programmes that simulate chemical reactions, voting behaviour for different samples of a population, moves made by hockey or football players, and many more.

Despite the apparent effectiveness of such programmes, they are heavily outnumbered by the more straightforward tutorial and drill and practice material. This is partly because of the difficulty of writing simulations: the complexity of the programming involved means that they are generally beyond the scope of the 'amateur'. Indeed the course-authoring systems now being sold by many computer manufacturers to encourage preparation of educational programmes are for the most part tailored exclusively to tutorial or drill and practice types of instruction.

In summary, computer-based learning, especially when used with microcomputers, appears to have considerable potential. Good computer-based instructional programmes – especially simulations – fulfil several of the requirements we have specified for lifelong learning, such as active learner involvement and the possibility of simulating real-world situations. These features of good CAI stand to benefit all students in higher education, but they have special implications for those learners who may have only limited access to formal educational establishments. Although this group presently represents a minority of students involved in higher education, some commentators have forecast that studying at a distance will eventually become the norm, and that the traditional school or university may eventually be rendered obsolete. For example, Masuda (1981) has described an information society in which computer communications technology will bring about the automation of knowledge-related services and operations, humans will be increasingly released from the need to work for subsistence, which in turn will increase leisure and lead to much greater involvement in learning activities. Masuda further argues that learning will take place primarily by computer-based systems, and that 'education will be freed from the restrictions of income, time, and place' (p. 65), with unlimited educational opportunities and conditions that make it possible for people to develop their full educational potential.

Hence education in the future, according to Masuda, will move out of the control of normal educational institutions, and be concentrated instead on individual learners, linked to each other in knowledge networks. Furthermore, it follows that this type of self-directed, individually tailored learning will not be restricted to the conventional years of schooling, but will be lifelong – 'to enable adults and elderly people to adapt themselves to the changes of the information society' (p. 67). Based upon the limited evidence available so far, it would appear that present versions of computer-based instruction fall far short of what Masuda might expect of them in the information society of the future. Furthermore, forecasts about the demise of the school and university tend to ignore the complex social functions that these institutions fulfil.

Computers and distance education

Whether or not computers succeed in transforming educational systems in the ways that have been suggested, it remains true that computer-assisted instruction has so far had only a marginal impact upon teaching and learning in higher education. Furthermore, the use of computers in distance education has scarcely begun. While there is great interest in exploring ways in which computers might be used to free distance learners from the constraints of having to study in special places or at special times, there is no general agreement so far about how this could be done most effectively. For example, it may be that computer-based learning materials could in the future take the place of textbooks or study modules, and audio-tapes, that are presently distributed through the post. As yet, however, only a very limited amount of material of this kind has been developed, and the pedagogical superiority of available computer-based learning materials has by no means been established. A number of commercial publishers are actively involved in developing computer-based learning material, which they hope to sell in much the same way that textbooks have been marketed. Although it is not clear to what extent such programmes will embody the instructional principles that would be most relevant for promotion of lifelong learning, some of the most successful commercial programmes in Britain, aimed at the elementary and secondary school, have been of the simulation type.

In contrast to the use of computers as a delivery device for course material, other possible applications include computer-based systems to link distant learners together in a form of computer conference or network. This is an interesting application of the technology, in that the computer is in effect being used to foster social interaction instead of encouraging the individualisation that is stressed with so much CAI. Advantages of linking learners together electronically in this way (as opposed to, say, by means of the traditional telephone-based tele-conferencing) include the fact that participants do not all have to be logged on at the same time, but can enter or leave the system when it is convenient; messages are not limited to those passing between instructor and student, but can involve student-to-student communication by individuals or groups, and such interchanges can be public or private. Unlike the telephone, the computer will make a record of the communications as they take place. Already there are more than 20 such conferencing systems (and thousands of individual conferences) in North America, many of which are based upon home microcomputers. Costs vary, but can be substantially lower for communication time than is the case with the telephone. A further development will undoubtedly be the supplementing of textual information by graphic displays,

151

although none of the commercially available systems allow this at present.

By using this type of network capability, computer technology might be used to service distance learners with electronic delivery of learning material (examinations, instructors' comments on previously completed work, homework exercises, and so on). Digitised information that can be interpreted by a microcomputer, can be transmitted by telephone, cable, or even FM radio and it is easily recorded on a diskette or cassette tape. Several institutions are in fact experimenting with approaches that might supplement the basic instruction offered in distance learning courses. So far, however, experience with alternative systems is so limited that it is not clear exactly how – or even whether – computers can best be used for remote learners. Although traditional materials, such as books and course manuals, have proved resilient over many years, it seems plausible that the new information technology could in the future provide a valuable means for expanding the channels of communication available to the distance learner – or for that matter to students in general.

In this connection, the University of Waterloo has for several years used electronic communication as a component of its distance education programme. For example, in an introductory computer science course students are loaned a lap-top computer (mailed to them with other more traditional course materials) and return their assignments via electronic mail, using a modem linked to the telephone system. The instructor's comments are returned to students the same way, and those enroled in the course are also able to communicate with each other, and the university, using a type of computer conferencing. Submitting assignments this way overcomes the delay that occurs when relying on the mail service, and enables students to obtain virtually instant feedback on their work (Black, Cowan, Dyck, Fenton, Knapper, and Stepien, 1988). Perhaps for this reason the course is extremely popular and completion rates have been very high (in excess of 90 per cent) compared to many distance courses. A number of other institutions have used computer conferencing to support distance education, for example the British Open University, the University of Guelph and the Ontario Institute for Studies in Education (see, for example, Harasim, 1990; McConnell, 1990).

In September 1990 the National Interactive Video Centre in London presented a concept for the application of technology in education called 'Multimedia'. It combines television, stereo sound and computers, and is intended to replace textbooks with a type of electronic simulation. Philips, Sony and Matsushita are collaborating on the commercial development of the idea, and hope to bring it on to the market in 1992. To take an example cited at the launch, a person learning photography could try out different camera settings for recording a particular scene. The scene is presented on television, and the camera is simulated on a home computer. Using the keyboard, the student can instruct the computer to 'develop' the picture and to see the result on TV. In this way the learner can practise and experiment with many types of exposure and development times without the mess of using real chemicals, darkroom, or even a camera. The designers claim that the system is especially useful for people with little background in the topic being taught – apparently because the learners are so active (compared to instruction from print or in a classroom), and the system so engaging and flexible. The advocates also claim there will be significant cost savings compared to traditional instruction.

In the comments made above, the term computer-assisted instruction is used in a rather narrow sense to refer to instruction that is generally complete in itself, does not require any special computing skills on the part of the student, and deals with subject matter outside the field of computing itself. In other words, in CAI the computer is used as an instructional delivery mechanism. We have mentioned above that although CAI has a long history, its present use within education in general, and higher education in particular, has been limited. This is not to say, however, that students in higher education institutions only rarely come into contact with computers in their day-to-day learning – quite the contrary. In many North American and European universities students from a wide range of disciplines learn a variety of computer-related skills as part of their regular academic courses. In contrast to CAI, however, these skills are directly related to computing itself, and involve either programming, computer-based technology or use of computers as a tool (for example in statistical calculation).

Computer literacy

The notion of 'computer literacy' as a basic requirement for all graduates of the education system has been widely discussed in many countries (see Knapper and Wills, 1983). There appears to be general agreement that the educated citizens of tomorrow should be knowledgeable about computers in the same way that they should be literate and 'numerate'. There is also agreement that this requirement can no longer be confined to the disciplines that have traditionally used computers, such as mathematics and engineering. There is much less agreement, however, on the precise components of computer literacy. At one time learning about computers was almost inevitably associated with learning to use a programming language (such as PASCAL or FORTRAN), and this is still a requirement for a great many students, especially in the science and technology areas. The rationale here is that mastering programming skills has a utility in itself, and is also valuable in learning basic problem-solving skills that can be transferred to a wide variety of situations. If this were true, teaching programming would be an essential component of a lifelong education curriculum. Unfortunately, however, there is as yet little empirical support for the second contention and, meanwhile, rapidly evolving technology continues to change the way in which human beings interact with the computer. Hence the argument has been made that computer literacy is not equivalent to sophistication in programming, but involves other components such as an understanding of the logic, function, and different applications of computer systems, and a grasp of the wider social implications of information technology. This is reflected in curriculum changes in computer science courses. For example, the introductory course in computing at the University of Waterloo, required in most departments across the university, has changed from an almost exclusive emphasis on programming to teaching a wide range of practical applications, such as word processing, use of spread-sheets and data-base management, among others (see Dyck, Black, Cowan, and Fenton, 1988).

Knapper (1988c) directly tackled the question of to what extent educational technology might be said to fulfil criteria for lifelong learning, such as those spelled out in Chapter 3. He selected eight crucial characteristics of the learning process against which to assess the possible contribution of technology:

- *activity* (learners cannot be simply passive consumers of wisdom served up by teachers);
- *democracy* (learning must be largely self-directed);
- *flexibility* (learning must take place at a variety of times and in a variety of places);
- *collaboration* (learning requires team work and communication skills);

- *regard for individual differences* (individual learning styles and goals must be taken into account);
- *relevance* (learning must be related to real life);
- *integration* (formal learning must take account of knowledge from different fields and in real world settings);
- *protection from fear of loss of status* (adult learners must feel competent and in control).

As was pointed out in the section on distance learning, these learning criteria are also important in conventional education with traditional learners. However, they are absolutely vital in the case of lifelong learning, because of the special needs and characteristics of adult students.

Knapper went on to apply these criteria to various forms of educational technology. He concluded, for instance, that computer simulation encourages active learning, is highly flexible, makes learning relevant and avoids embarrassment. By contrast, computer conferencing has all these advantages and in addition promotes collaboration. Computer-assisted learning is not at all democratic, allows little integration of material from different areas, and offers little chance of collaborative learning, although it is very flexible, demands a great deal of activity from the learner, and makes it possible to avoid embarrassment, even when problems are encountered. Knapper's evaluation of instructional technology makes it plain that, at least from the point of view of lifelong learning, not all applications of technology to education are equally desirable. The criteria just outlined offer teachers and planners in higher education a useful framework for assessing the possible utility of different technology-based instructional approaches.

While arguments about appropriate uses of technology will no doubt continue in the future, it can be said with assurance that the computer will occupy an increasingly central role in the day-to-day work and leisure time of most individuals, especially in modern industrial societies. Hence knowing *about* computers and information technology is as important for the effective lifelong learner as the opportunity to learn *with and from* computers. Already many institutions of higher education have a considerable range of computing equipment on campus: some private universities in the United States even require students to purchase a personal computer when they are admitted (see Farrell, 1983; Turner, 1983). It remains to be seen, however, whether this equipment will be used in ways that will allow students from a variety of disciplines to understand both the potential and the limitations of information technology and to make sensible decisions in the future about how technology can best be used in the service of their own lives and society. Indeed, if forecasts about a new knowledge-based society come true in the way suggested by Masuda and others, it is clear that this could have profound implications for the structure of power and democracy within society, since those who understand the information processing and delivery systems will have effective control over those who do not. This would seem to imply that a crucial role for education is to teach students to understand technology, but also to use it wisely for the common good, not solely in the service of a future 'computocracy.'

Changing the system

We have focused until now primarily on teaching and learning in higher education. However, the task of promoting lifelong learning skills would involve the whole educational system, as we discussed in Chapter 4. Paradoxically, although institutions of higher education function in a world that is rapidly evolving, universities and colleges themselves are often slow to respond, and introducing many of the changes implied by a move to lifelong education is likely to encounter many obstacles.

Change strategies

One barrier to effecting change is likely to be the conservative institutional climate that prevails in many colleges and universities with respect to instructional methods (see Chapter 4). Little (1983) has suggested a number of strategies for introducing teaching innovations into higher education. Firstly, he recommends efforts to support individual initiatives by identifying staff who are likely – and able – to act as educational entrepreneurs. A second strategy is to 'cut one's losses' by ignoring the small number of teachers who will be adamantly opposed to innovation under any circumstances, and instead give support to those who can lead innovation effectively. Thirdly, Little advocates that those interested in promoting change should work directly with students, who often welcome the opportunity to make their learning experiences more meaningful and relevant – although he may underestimate the ability of the secondary school system to encourage student preferences for passive, traditional teaching approaches.

Lindquist (1978b) and Berg and Ostergren (1977) have suggested factors that can aid the introduction of innovation into educational settings. These include:

- *linkage* (bringing people together and confronting them with new information and ideas);
- *openness* (active searching for new ideas and information);
- *gain/loss* (providing rewards of security and personal satisfaction or self-realisation);
- *ownership* (giving individuals a stake in initiating and developing the innovation);
- *leadership and power* (sustaining and institutionalising the innovation).

Mathias and Rutherford (1983) attempted to make use of these strategies in an innovation at the University of Birmingham that involved pairs of academic staff evaluating each other's courses on a voluntary basis. Their assessment of the scheme provided support for the model of educational innovation proposed by Lindquist and Berg and Ostergren.

Changes in institutional policy

Moves toward change can only succeed if there is support from leaders in higher education, along with administrative structures that will facilitate lifelong learning. The latter include many of the characteristics of institutional organisation reviewed in Chapters 3 and 4, such as flexible logistical arrangements for timetabling and for provision and use of physical space, appropriate services for mature students and a general emphasis on quality of learning as opposed to more easily quantifiable indices, such as the number of hours a class meets for formal lectures. Other crucial aspects of administrative procedures concern systems of assessment (reviewed in detail in Chapter 4), opportunities for group and peer learning, team teaching and interdisciplinary courses.

Finally, there is the whole matter of the institutional reward system, which in many colleges and universities is heavily weighted in favour of staff involvement in scholarship and research. If lifelong learning is to be encouraged, then it is essential that energy devoted to the improvement of teaching and learning be rewarded by the same tokens (tenure, promotion, in some cases merit pay) as are now accorded for demonstrated scholarship. Furthermore, there needs to be a recognition that research on teaching and learning itself is every bit as valid a scholarly contribution as more traditional research within the bounds of the discipline. At too many institutions today it appears that research on the teaching and learning of chemistry, as opposed to research in chemistry itself, constitutes a less significant contribution to the work of the department and institution. Indeed Knapper's studies of attitudes to the institutional reward system in Canada and Australia indicate that members of faculty perceive traditional research to be given twice the weight accorded to teaching, despite what it may be stated in official policies. This is regarded as a major obstacle to enhancing the quality of teaching or introducing new instructional methods (Knapper, 1988a, 1990).

Changes in national policy

Such changes in institutional policy may in turn require a shift in philosophy at an even higher level, such as the ministry of education, grants commission, accreditation agency or similar body. Despite the considerable autonomy which individual universities and colleges often enjoy, national education policies have in some cases had profound effects upon the organisation of higher education in relation to the concerns that are the focus of this book.

One recent British example is the 'Enterprise in Higher Education' scheme developed by the Training Agency of the Department of Employment. Institutions of higher education make proposals to the agency for funding of teaching and curriculum development schemes. Such schemes must involve making the skills and knowledge of new graduates more compatible with those needed to function successfully in industry. Many of the measures proposed involve periods of work in industrial settings, while others have emphasised project work and 'learning to learn' skills. The scheme is expected to arouse sufficient support in industry to permit the ending of government funding after a five-year introductory period. By November 1989 32 contracts had been awarded to 14 universities, 12 polytechnics, four colleges of further education and two consortia, some involving budgets of up to a million pounds.

In another British government intervention, the Secretary of State for Education in 1989 outlined the a new national policy of mass higher education. It was proposed to open the higher education system to new groups of learners, among them people without traditional entry qualifications or beyond the conventional age limits. Strategies for accomplishing these objectives include orientation workshops for non-traditional students, adult learning support centres, procedures for accreditation of prior learning, developmental assessment and support from developmental mentors (Schlossberg, 1990).

Other famous examples of major educational policy initiatives include the Robbins report in Britain and the Swedish Educational Reform. In some cases too it is a political decision by a national government that has established specific institutions that may exemplify some of the principles of lifelong education. The creation of the British Open University by Harold Wilson's Labour Government is a case in point. There are other instances, however, where initiatives of this sort have been successfully resisted. For example, reaction to the 1983 Leverhulme report from the British vice-chancellors made it evident that implementation of its key recommendations would face formidable obstacles.

On the other hand, academics can themselves often affect national policy, for instance by working through professional associations, many of which have been actively involved in promoting discussions of teaching and learning by holding conferences, publishing journals, and setting up policy committees. Certainly, it seems likely that if academics themselves do not play a leading role in promoting effective learning skills in students, the initiative may slip from their grasp. Already in the United States, for example, an increasing proportion of higher education is being offered by institutions outside the formal education establishment, such as the growing number of 'colleges' set up by large industrial and commercial concerns – many of which are officially accredited to give degrees, some even up to the doctorate. For example, Donne (1983) has reported that the total budget for training and development in industry in the United States amounts to 80 to 100 billion dollars a year (compared to about 60 billion dollars spent by that country's three thousand colleges and universities), and that the American Telephone and Telegraph Company conglomerate alone spends approximately 1.3 billion dollars a year for this purpose. These activities involve about 700,000 full- and part-time educators.

Niebuhr (1982) has referred to this trend in terms of post-secondary education's 'disaggregating'. He estimates that 46 million students get their education through institutions outside the formal education system and that the growth of these competitive educational activities is tied to the recognition that learning is instrumental to economic and institutional performance. This presents a formidable challenge to traditional higher education to examine its goals, methods and future directions, with a view to meeting the needs of learners more effectively in a rapidly changing world.

Recapitulation

New approaches to higher education, exemplified by distance learning institutions and experimental colleges and universities, are already grappling with the problem of providing appropriate learning opportunities for a much broader range of students with distinctive skills and motivations. Emerging understanding of how students may be better equipped to become autonomous, self-directed learners could build upon existing programmes for enhancing learning skills and improving teaching methods. Instructional technology, which has had a long and rather disappointing history, has the potential to broaden access to higher education and to change the nature of learning itself. Transforming universities and colleges to a system that will promote lifelong education, however, will require the adoption of a common goal that focuses on the *process* of learning instead of just the content. There will also be a need to assess just how well this goal is being attained. How this assessment may be carried out is the topic addressed in the next chapter.

7 Evaluating lifelong education

The importance of evaluation

The terms 'evaluation', 'appraisal' and 'assessment' have cropped up repeatedly in our discussions so far, reflecting the central role of evaluation in any educational system. For example, we argued in Chapter 4 that the assessment of students (by means of examinations and grading procedures) is perhaps the greatest single influence on student learning in formal institutions of higher education, even if its importance often goes unrecognised by instructors. We have also discussed student evaluation of courses and instructors, which we have argued is an important component in the process of staff development leading to innovation and change in teaching methods. Elsewhere in the book we have touched on the appraisal of particular institutions, learning approaches and support systems for lifelong education. In other words the topic of evaluation is a recurring theme throughout these pages. The present chapter picks up the threads of these earlier discussions and focuses on the evaluation of procedures and approaches that aim to promote lifelong learning – hence the focus is on lifelong education itself.

One aim in the book has been to make a case for the importance of fostering lifelong learning prerequisites and skills in students: we thus devoted the early chapters to a theoretical conception of a system of higher education based on lifelong learning principles. Our argument was based upon philosophical, social and, in part, political premises, which we believe will be shared by many educators. However, whether or not this is so, it is important to recognise that our beliefs about the importance of lifelong education are in themselves not amenable to empirical evaluation. A second aim of the book has been to outline what kind of practical changes in higher education might lead to the promotion of lifelong learning. An evaluation of the relevant procedures and methods, using lifelong education principles as appropriate criteria, *is* possible. What we shall do in the remainder of the book, then, is to try to evaluate some of the practical attempts at introducing lifelong learning methods in colleges and universities – especially approaches that have been described in the previous two chapters. A major focus here is thus to examine how such developments might be judged, as well as to describe some of the types of evaluation that have been carried out. This should shed light on the question of whether the institutions and innovations concerned do indeed produce in students the skills, personal characteristics and values that we have claimed are essential for effective lifelong learning.

It is possible to identify two broad approaches to this issue. The first involves the assessment of individuals, usually students, and the second focuses on evaluation of systems and programmes related to lifelong education. These two approaches are not of course mutually exclusive: indeed, to study the effectiveness of a programme it is often necessary to assess the students who are taking part. It is important to bear in mind, however, that such assessment is primarily of value because of the light it sheds upon the programme and the pointers it may provide for change and improvement – not as a type of 'summative evaluation' of the students being tested.

Difficulties of evaluation

The topic of educational evaluation is one that has been dealt with exhaustively in the professional literature, and it is not possible to do more here than sketch out some of the ways in which evaluations have been conducted, and draw attention to the stumbling blocks that will be encountered in any attempt to carry out assessments of procedures that aim to promote lifelong learning. It is important to review these obstacles, however, if only to explain the relative dearth of good evaluative studies in the area.

The first difficulty in the evaluation of lifelong learning approaches is that many of the teaching methods that might be expected to be relevant (for example those reviewed in Chapter 5) were not necessarily developed within a lifelong education framework. This means that evaluation criteria relevant to the sorts of objectives laid out in earlier chapters have in many cases not been articulated. An innovation may be introduced for many different reasons – for example to save instructional time, or to cope with an institutional problem such as lack of suitably qualified instructors. Hence, if an evaluation takes place, the data gathered may not reflect students' acquisition of lifelong learning skills, but instead deal with outcomes such as time spent on the learning task, success on a multiple-choice examination, and preference for this method over a conventional lecture approach. It is not that these outcomes are necessarily unimportant, but rather that they are not in themselves adequate criteria for deciding whether or not a particular teaching approach fulfils the more complex goals that we regard as important. This limitation applies to some instructional approaches more than others. For example, in the case of instructional technology the goal is often one of providing a more 'efficient' system of teaching, and criteria for success often involve achieving the outcomes of conventional instruction, but with demonstration of a greater amount of learning, at less cost, and in a shorter time.

In the case of other innovations, such as guided design, the theoretical underpinnings of the approach do specify objectives of more relevance to our present purposes, such as enhanced problem-solving skills and more autonomous learning. Even here, however, the existing research is frequently inadequate to instil confidence that students have developed appropriate lifelong learning attitudes and skills – developing measures of autonomous, self-directed learning is a difficult business.

Ideally, the research should be of a longitudinal nature, in which the progress of a cadre of students is monitored over time, to examine not just immediate effects at the end of a course but also whether, and how, students build upon their learning experience in subsequent courses and in their later careers. In the case of lifelong education this is especially important, since many of the desired outcomes might only become apparent many years after the initial learning took place. Longitudinal research is, however, notoriously difficult to conduct, and there is a paucity of studies of this sort in education in general, let alone in the area of lifelong education. Long term research is expensive, presents difficulties in maintaining contact with the students involved, and requires specially trained investigators. Given the fact that many of the innovations described here were developed not by educational researchers but by practising teachers with other more pressing responsibilities, it is hardly surprising that a good many innovations have not been evaluated at all, or have been studied rather superficially on a 'one shot' basis.

Another major difficulty is that of controlling all the variables affecting learning outcomes. For example, some studies of educational innovations have demonstrated change in the participating students (in terms of increased learning, different attitudes and values, etc.), but there is no way of telling whether similar changes might have taken place if the learners had been exposed to traditional types of instruction. Other studies have used control groups in which the progress of students' learning during exposure to some unconventional procedure is compared with outcomes for students who remained in the traditional environment. A major problem with such studies, however, is that learners are very rarely randomly assigned to the experimental and control groups. In circumstances where students voluntarily select a particular type of learning, it seems quite likely that they would have different attitudes and motivations compared to learners who opt for conventional instructional approaches. Even in those studies where some attempt is made to provide a control for this factor (by random assignment to groups or careful matching in terms of a wide range of variables), there is the possibility that various motivational factors can arise within the experimental group simply because they are the object of special attention (the so-called Hawthorne effect). This possibly accounts for the fact that in the early years of an innovation many studies seem to show its superiority over conventional instruction. This was certainly true for programmed instruction, Keller Plan teaching and many types of educational technology. (Another reason, of course, is that research which fails to show a superiority does not get published.)

On the other hand, some studies may underestimate the effectiveness of the new technique, simply because the interest surrounding the experiment causes special efforts to be made even by the control group. For example, in some of the early British studies of the effectiveness of teaching machines, students in both the experimental and control groups appeared to be learning particularly well. Detailed examination of the 'traditional' lessons revealed in some cases that they had been planned with much greater care than usual: the necessity of specifying instructional objectives for the project and of planning careful tests of student learning had presumably caused teachers to think about lesson planning and to structure their material in a way that was different from normal practice.

Not only can all these factors operate in individual studies, but they can also colour the general picture that emerges from overviews of research on a particular innovation. Even meta-analysis, which was devised specifically as a means of summarising conclusions from a broad range of studies, is not immune from these problems (see Slavin, 1983). This technique, which has been widely applied to studies of educational innovations, aims to extract the commonalities in published research reports in order to permit generalisations about whether, and under what circumstances, particular treatment effects can be demonstrated. Especially in more recent meta-analyses, an attempt is generally made to exclude research that is methodologically unsound or inappropriate in some other respect. This is certainly a great improvement on the earlier analyses that often gathered research studies on an indiscriminate basis, regardless of methodological flaws. Whatever the approach used, however, it is difficult to compensate for many of the problems listed earlier, such as the failure to report negative results, the Hawthorne effect, and the lack of longitudinal data, among others.

Yet another difficulty that plagues research in this area is that of proving a link between the 'treatment' and the measured outcome. For example, students who participate in a particular type of education may indeed demonstrate enhanced learning, distinctive values and increased motivation, compared to a matching group of students who were taught in a different way. Assuming that some of the previously mentioned methodological difficulties had been overcome, it is still extremely difficult to be sure that the differences observed are really attributable to the different types of educational experience: differences in outcomes could be due to factors that are quite unknown to the investigators. While this problem exists in all studies outside the laboratory, the problem increases as the complexity of the research setting increases. Hence it may be plausible to talk about controlling most of the variables in a small scale study of a particular innovation (such as a peer learning component of an introductory sociology class), but in cases where a whole course or programme is involved, so many factors could potentially affect students' experiences that attributing changes in behaviour or attitudes to a particular learning method becomes problematical at best.

Despite these cautionary comments, the fact that it is often difficult to evaluate educational programmes and determine precisely their long term effects on students does not mean that attempts at evaluation should simply be abandoned. On the contrary, we believe that it is essential to monitor relevant educational developments on a continuing basis. We believe further that such evaluation needs to be of a 'formative' nature, whereby the system, institution or innovation can

165

be assessed on an on-going basis, with a view to revealing those aspects that appear to be successful in promoting lifelong learning as well as factors that mitigate against it. In other words we would wish to broaden the approach to assessment of lifelong learning programmes to emphasise not simply a retrospective and summative judgement on whether the programme 'worked' or was 'better' than the traditional programme, but also to include formative evaluation that could provide information rich enough to *improve* the programme. This is especially important when the data gathered include information on student performance: these data should be seen not primarily as a comment on the students' inherent abilities, but as an indication of what sort of learning took place and how it was facilitated by the instructional activities and educational context.

In view of the difficulties of carrying out valid evaluations, it is often tempting for educators, especially those involved with educational change, to shrug their shoulders and abandon evaluation as too complex to be worth the effort and time that might otherwise be devoted to the project itself. We urge, however, that this would be a mistake. Even in the absence of a formal assessment system, it is inevitable that informal evaluation will take place, based largely on subjective impressions by students, teachers and others. Although such impressions are often very inaccurate, they can be extremely powerful in guiding public opinion on the achievements of a project. Given that evaluation will take place, it is preferable that it be based on reasonably objective information and judged against appropriate criteria, rather than on mere hearsay or gossip.

The results of evaluation

In earlier chapters we have reviewed a number of educational innovations that seem to hold out the promise of fostering or improving lifelong learning skills. Many of the instructional approaches we have described, such as peer learning, computer-aided instruction and project methods, have been written about at length in the educational literature. Quite reasonably, a question that frequently arises in connection with any innovation asks what evidence exists for the effectiveness of the new approach compared to existing instructional methods. In view of the difficulties of carrying out definitive studies of the effects of instruction on learning, it is not surprising that much of the evidence for the effectiveness of approaches reviewed here is lacking, or has serious shortcomings. Thus we cannot turn to the research literature and find large numbers of carefully designed evaluations that provide precise guidance on choosing teaching methods for particular students, for particular learning goals, or in particular social contexts. Rather, the picture that emerges from reviewing the educational research literature reveals a large number of developments and innovations implemented in relative isolation, sometimes not evaluated at all, sometimes assessed with good intentions but amateurish methods and often appraised incompletely. Hence those who look to particular instructional approaches as a way of implementing a deeply held educational philosophy – such as one emphasising lifelong learning – may have to take a great deal on faith.

Although this may seem to constitute a rather fragile basis for suggesting radical change in educational practice, it is important to bear in mind that the research evidence for the effectiveness of many traditional approaches to teaching is also equivocal or, in some cases, seems to demonstrate the limitations of traditional practices. In the latter category is much of the research on the lecture method (reviewed in Chapter 4), which seems to show that lectures are an ineffective way of promoting higher-order conceptual skills, changing attitudes, or fostering personal and social adjustment (Bligh, 1972). And the longitudinal studies by Gow and Kember (1990), Ramsden and Entwistle (1981) and Watkins (1984), mentioned in Chapter 4, show that most students in conventional universities may actually develop *less* sophisticated approaches to learning over the life of their undergraduate programmes. Given this negative scenario, it seems reasonable to experiment with teaching methods that can serve as alternatives to the lecture, even if evidence for their superiority is incomplete.

To cite an even more far-reaching example than the lecture method, the whole notion of the liberal arts curriculum (discussed at some length in Chapter 2) carries with it certain assumptions about the effects of this educational philosophy on student learning, attitudes and values. Although some serious attempts have been made to assess the effects of college education (e.g. Astin, 1977; Bowen, 1977), the research is limited by the same methodological difficulties that affect investigations into alternative educational approaches. In other words, we are arguing here that research on the effects of education is difficult, especially where we are seeking to demonstrate learning abilities that are sophisticated, are manifested in a wide variety of different ways and persist and develop over a lifetime. These difficulties exist for both innovative educational approaches and also for traditional methods, which is partly why the benefits of contemporary education are often a matter of faith.

Given these caveats, what conclusions can be drawn from the existing evidence about the effectiveness of some of the alternative approaches described in earlier chapters? In Chapter 5, for example, we have talked about distance education as a means of opening the doors of universities and colleges to a much broader cross-section of students. Some aspects of these developments can be evaluated in a fairly straightforward manner – for instance to determine how many non-traditional students actually enrol, how many of them complete programmes, and how well they perform in comparison to 'regular' students. Indeed, there are many studies of this kind: much less common, however, is research into the effects of such programmes on student learning, attitudes and values – especially long term effects.

Student learning styles

Despite the problems that beset educational research, efforts to understand learning processes continue. Of particular relevance to lifelong education are the recent attempts to examine what might be termed the 'anthropology' or 'phenomenology' of learning, by means of naturalistic in-depth studies of how students go about this task, the factors in the academic environment that influence their approach to academic study, and the cognitive changes that take place in students during their years at college and university. This research, instead of focusing upon the *content* of learning (which was the primary interest of early psychological investigations in the field), tries to describe the different ways in which students understand and structure the information, concepts and principles they encounter in their courses.

Among the earliest research of this sort was the series of longitudinal studies carried out at Harvard by Perry (see Perry, 1970), who postulated a developmental model of learning in which students can progress from an 'absolutistic' view of knowledge (seeking the 'right answers'), to a more relativistic way of reasoning, and eventually to the development of personal commitment and the ability to take responsibility for personal choice. In the context of mathematics and science learning, Resnick (1983) has taken up a similar theme in observing that many students who do well on textbook problems are often unable to apply the laws and formulae they have mastered to the interpretation of real physical events. Beginning students tend to use their own 'naive' theories to explain real-world phenomena and may still resort to these theories in attempting to solve new problems that lie outside the scope of textbook examples. Arguing that learners persist in trying to 'construct' understanding and are dissatisfied with simply mirroring what they are told or what they read, Resnick argues that successful problem solving in science and mathematics requires a type of 'qualitative reasoning' in which alternative relationships among variables must be carefully considered. Unless teaching recognises these qualitative aspects, and students are guided to make sense out of procedures and formulae, it will be impossible to achieve the problem-solving skills that most academics see as desirable. A similar argument is made by Brown et al. (1989) in their criticism of 'decontextualised' learning that takes place in most classrooms. As explained in Chapter 2, Brown and his colleagues call for introduction of more 'authentic' learning, and suggest an approach for achieving this that they call 'cognitive apprenticeship'.

The British psychologist Pask (1976) offers some insights into this dilemma with his account of the different ways in which students attempt to build structures to explain the concepts and phenomena they encounter. He distinguishes between 'serialists' and 'holists' (Pask's original terms were rather more evocative: holistic learners were referred to as 'lumpers' and serialists as 'stringers'). Serialists concentrate on one aspect of the task at a time in a stepwise fashion, and advance only simple hypotheses to explain what they perceive; holists look for whole structures and use more complex hypotheses in which several aspects of the problem are considered simultaneously.

While Pask was concerned with student performance at learning *tasks*, Marton and his associates at the University of Gothenburg in Sweden have focused on students' approaches to study in their handling of learning *materials*. Their research makes use of interviews, diaries, and similar techniques. Marton distinguishes between a 'deep' approach to studying and a 'surface' approach. In the deep approach the student actively strives for meaning and understanding in order to make sense of what has been learned, tries to identify central principles and ideas, relates concepts and arguments to evidence and data, and forges links with previous knowledge and experience. In the surface approach there is a passive concern with rote learning, memorisation, isolated details and facts, in order to reproduce the material rather than understand it:

such learners may solve problems, but in a mechanical way that may often be inappropriate. To give an example mentioned by Marton and Saljo (1976a; 1976b), students studying a text with a surface approach focused on the words of the text rather than on the underlying message. In contrast, students adopting a deep approach seemed to focus their attention beyond or beneath the text in an attempt to identify the basic ideas being presented. These ideas have clear relevance for our earlier discussion (Chapter 4) about the frequent discrepancy between the high-level teaching objectives espoused by many university teachers and the more trivial types of learning performance often required in examinations. In this context, it is interesting to note that students who are capable of functioning at a deep level may not trouble to do so if the demands of the situation encourage surface level performance, as demonstrated by the work of Watkins (1984) and Ramsden and Entwistle (1981), mentioned earlier.

Miller and Parlett (1974) introduced the notion of cue-seeking in students. 'Cue-seekers' actively look for all the hints they can obtain about what is required in a learning (or examination) situation, and successfully adapt to the demands of the 'hidden curriculum'. 'Cue-conscious' students are able to do this too, but have a more critical and independent approach and can demonstrate deep learning if required to do so. Miller and Parlett's third unfortunate category of the 'cue-deaf' refers to students who are simply not aware that there are any cues to respond to.

Another research team that adopted a similar approach was the Study Methods Group at the British Open University (see Morgan, Taylor, and Gibbs, 1982), who followed a group of 29 students enroled in an introductory social science course, interviewing them on three occasions to probe various aspects of their learning experience. They were able to identify differences consistent with the Gothenburg group's distinction between deep and surface approaches to study. Morgan and his colleagues recommend that educators design activities and methods of student self-assessment that would encourage learners to engage in more deep level, active ways of studying, and to change their conceptions of the learning task if necessary. They caution however that this goal will be frustrated if university teaching neglects the important task of developing appropriate study skills, and urge the development of models of learning that are based upon a sympathy for the student's perspective, as opposed to experts' notions of appropriate discipline-based knowledge and skills.

Marton (1983) has argued that 'the very amount of textual material assigned to students makes an extreme surface approach impossible' (p. 328). He also makes the point that a good deal of learning is interpersonal, and that students quickly learn to recognise which of their teachers are convergent thinkers and which are more likely to encourage the type of critical approach inherent in deep learning. As Hounsell (1983) and Ramsden (1982) have pointed out, faced with an overloaded syllabus and assessment procedures that stress powers of memory rather than understanding, students may be discouraged from deep and critical thinking. An important factor here is the general departmental ethos in which students find themselves, which can have profound effects upon methods of study. In particular, inappropriate assessment techniques, excessive workloads, and an unduly restricted framework of choice in learning are likely to have a negative impact upon the way students go about the learning task (Ramsden and Entwistle, 1981; Watkins, 1984).

Accepting that these factors may well inhibit lifelong learning skills and attitudes, it is of considerable interest to ask whether or not inappropriate learning can be changed by timely interventions on the part of teaching staff or others concerned with effective study techniques. Ramsden (1982) cautions that 'no amount of attention to teaching and assessment can guarantee that students will take deep approaches: in the end it's up to them' (p. 5). On the other hand, Raaheim and Wankowski (1981) describe a small-scale experiment that provides at least tentative evidence for a relationship between participation in a study skills programme and problem-solving ability.

Before leaving the topic of appropriate student learning skills, it is worth speculating briefly upon views of knowledge and learning that may be held by teachers in higher education. This is a topic that has received very little investigation – perhaps because undergraduates provide a much more amenable population of subjects for investigation than do academic staff. However, Beers and Bloomingdale (1983) have investigated the epistemological beliefs of college teachers, using a framework similar to that suggested by Perry. They conclude that the system of values and beliefs held by instructors involves many attributions about student difficulties in learning – for example some teachers may ascribe student learning problems to inherent lack of talent or personality factors, while other instructors see the cause as lack of experience or opportunity. (Beers also discovered a relationship between discipline and the nature of course objectives, with lower-level objectives being associated with the natural sciences as opposed to the social sciences and humanities.) Since such attributions may cause some instructors to shrug their shoulders and 'give up' on unsuccessful students, this seems a topic that is ripe for further research. In this connection, Knapper (1988a; 1990) studied teaching-related attitudes of university faculty in Australia and Canada. He found that respondents espoused quite sophisticated learning objectives that were consistent with the principles of lifelong learning. However, there was also a tendency for teachers to see students as lacking learning skills needed to fulfil such objectives.

Effects of work/study programmes

An important area of interest in Chapter 5 was the forging of links between higher education institutions and the world of work. Although the benefits of experiential learning and cooperative education may seem self-evident to the proponents of lifelong education, it is more difficult to find empirical evidence for their effectiveness. One relevant study by Somers and Bridges (1982) investigated the effects of such programmes on post-graduate success of students, including personal development, subsequent employment opportunities and involvement in continuing education and graduate study. Results indicated that experiential education is seen as providing preparation for subsequent study that is equal to or better than traditional programmes, and that the graduates of non-traditional programmes have no particular difficulty in obtaining employment.

Hayes and Travis (1974) carried out a comprehensive national (USA) study of employer experience with cooperative programmes, sponsored by the United States Office of Education. The study was intended to provide a cost-benefit analysis of cooperative education, and obtained data from 70 employers based on their experience with several hundred coop students between 1964 and 1974. Results suggested that 'recruitment yield' (proportion of people hired as a percentage of those interviewed) was thirteen times higher for coop students than for college graduates in general, and that recruitment costs were on average dramatically lower for graduates of coop programmes than for other recent college graduates. Although there were no significant differences between employer ratings of work performance for coop students and other graduates, the former received more promotions to supervisory positions, and did so sooner than other college graduates.

Coop students were frequently offered and accepted jobs within the organisation that they had worked for during their programme, and the likelihood of their remaining with the firm was greater than for other graduates.

While such tangible benefits are clearly important, it is also necessary to examine the effects of work/study programmes on the *quality* of student learning (Breathnach, 1983). An early attempt to study the benefits of cooperative education was carried out in the 1960s, and involved a comparison of 22 cooperative programmes and 16 conventional programmes in a variety of USA higher education institutions (Wilson and Lyons, 1961). Data gathered were based upon interviews and opinion surveys with students, members of faculty and employers. The Committee concluded that cooperative education yielded the following benefits:

- links between theory and practice gave a greater meaning to study;
- student motivation for study was enhanced;
- students achieved a greater degree of personal independence, responsibility and maturity;
- students showed greater interpersonal skills;
- students were better able to understand the demands of the work situation;
- there was greater access to higher education by a broader range of students;
- there were closer contacts between academics and employers, with resultant benefits for curriculum planning;
- there was more efficient utilisation of institutional resources in higher education;
- cooperative education provided a means for business to attract and screen potential employees.

It is not clear that the study did indeed provide unequivocal evidence to support all these conclusions. Whereas some of the outcomes could be measured in fairly straightforward ways, others are more a matter of perception and opinion. Furthermore, a particular problem arises because of the self-selection of students who enter work/study programmes: such individuals are quite likely to place a high value on the unique characteristics of cooperative education, and thus it is not particularly surprising that they stress the benefits of their experience. Nonetheless, whether or not the conclusions reported by Wilson and

Lyons provide the empirical support for cooperative education that they claim, their list of outcomes certainly provides an exemplary set of criteria against which such programmes could be evaluated.

Evaluative studies of this sort show that there are definite economic benefits to students who participate in work/study programmes; the research also provides some evidence of academic achievement as measured by, for example, college or university grades. However, studies of cooperative education are hampered by the sorts of methodological difficulties reviewed at the beginning of this chapter. Furthermore they do not really speak to many of the criteria that we have emphasised as especially important for promotion of lifelong learning skills – such as, for example, demonstration of students' ability to learn from a variety of sources, evaluate their own efforts, plan and guide their own learning, choose among various learning approaches, and similar qualities.

Effects of instructional innovations

Chapter 5 also examined a variety of innovative teaching methods, including various approaches to individualising instruction, methods intended to promote independent learning, project work of various sorts and methods that stress learning from peers. Many of these instructional innovations have been the subject of numerous research studies; in many cases there have even been studies (meta-analyses) of the studies themselves. Pascarella, Duby, Terenzini, and Iverson (1983), in a longitudinal study carried out at a large American 'commuter' university, found that peer group interactions had significant effects on intellectual and personal growth, and there is evidence that the effect is even more marked for students who live on campus. This would seem to reflect the conventional wisdom that much learning in the outside world is based on informal contacts with colleagues. Indeed, a USA survey of 300 Honeywell managers from throughout the corporation found that only a small fraction of an individual's management techniques had been learned in the classroom, with perhaps 80 per cent of learning being derived from contact with other people (Broderick, 1983).

Collier (1980; 1983) has reviewed a large number of studies that examine the impact of peer learning techniques on the development of higher order skills. He concludes that there is some evidence that these approaches result in heightened student motivation and increased involvement with their academic work. There is also evidence that students are able to apply principles they have learned to new situations (for example in individual learning), synthesise diverse materials, and gain a more sophisticated and systematic approach to problem solving, including facility at interdisciplinary collaboration and the ability to deal with conflicting viewpoints. Other research has focused not just on whether peer group methods result in learning, but on the precise conditions under which peer learning is most effective for particular groups (e.g., Larson, Dansereau, and Goetz, 1983).

Benefits of peer group learning may not be restricted to the student. Several writers have commented on important advantages to the instructor or tutor. Indeed Annis (1983), in a study of peer tutoring in circumstances that resemble Goldschmid's learning cell, found that although both tutors and tutored showed content-specific and more general cognitive gains than students not involved in the tutoring process, the improvement was significantly greater for those acting as tutors. This seems to confirm the popular notion that the best way to learn something is to teach it. Bouton and Garth (1982) have argued that the effect of learning groups on altering the role of the teacher – from sole authority to resource and guide – can be of special benefit in allowing an instructor to truly observe, perhaps for the first time, the student learning that takes place in the course. In this way, learning groups can become a spur to thinking about the nature of teaching and learning itself.

The McMaster University medical programme, which combines peer learning with project work (described in Chapter 5), has been the subject of extensive evaluation to assess the competencies of its graduates in relation to those of students from other, more traditional medical schools. There are regular entry and exit surveys of McMaster students, and data are collected annually from graduates of the programme. Performance on national licensing examinations is monitored, and records are maintained of the certification rate for graduates in the various medical specialties. In addition, the career paths and attitudes of students are systematically checked on a continuing basis. Data from these surveys are used not only to evaluate the success of the programme, but also as a basis for planning changes in curriculum and approaches to teaching. There is evidence that McMaster graduates (who write no formal examinations during their programme) perform close to the Canadian national average in licensing examinations, and have similar success rates in being accepted into internship and residency programmes compared to the graduates of other medical schools (Woodward and Neufeld, 1978). Surveys of graduating classes indicate that former students place a high value upon the problem-based orientation of the curriculum in preparing them for medical practice (see Ferrier et al., 1988). In view of the considerable difficulties in conducting research in this area (a matter that was reviewed earlier), such evidence provides encouraging support for the success of project-based instruction in promoting self-directed independent learning outside the university.

Despite the useful insights yielded by the studies reviewed above, a good deal of the research on educational innovations is rather unsatisfactory from the point of view of demonstrating that the approaches in question foster effective lifelong learning as we have defined it. Despite the plethora of research, most investigations focus on what, from the point of view of our preferred criteria, are rather narrow – or even trivial – learning outcomes, such as scores on multiple-choice tests, estimates of time taken in learning, and crude measures of students' preference for the instructional approach compared to traditional teaching, (see Knapper, 1980, for a fuller discussion). Some of the reasons for these inadequacies are easy to understand, and have been discussed above.

Effectiveness of special programmes and institutions

An underlying assumption of all higher education is that it will produce some type of change in students, and various attempts have been made by researchers to measure the effects of studying in college and university on subsequent behaviour and attitudes. Jacob (1957) reviewed a large body of empirical research, focusing particularly on the impact of universities and colleges on values, attitudes, and cognitive abilities – including a number of skills that are of direct relevance to lifelong learning, such as independent and critical thinking, emotional and aesthetic experience, 'liberal' attitudes, interpersonal sensitivity and similar factors. His conclusions were rather pessimistic (and caused considerable controversy in academic circles – see, for example, Barton, 1959). Jacob found that while some opinions change as a result of going to college, and while some colleges have a major impact on students' values, on the whole most basic values and cognitive skills do not change for most students at most institutions in a way that can be attributed to the teaching they have received. Barton

(1959), however, in an incisive critique, concluded that Jacob's findings were attributable primarily to the methodological problems that beset research of this type. More recently, Terenzini, Pascarella, and Lorang (1982), who used a sophisticated statistical approach to take account of effects of extraneous variables on student learning, reached the more optimistic conclusion that attendance at university did lead to cognitive gains that could not be attributed simply to normal maturation.

Turning to the topic of Chapter 6, in which we reviewed various mechanisms for facilitating lifelong learning in higher education institutions, there is a dearth of evidence that special programmes such as staff development and study skills services really do promote lifelong learning in students. In a sense, it would be surprising if there were definitive evidence, since most of the 'facilitating mechanisms' we reviewed were not specifically put in place to fulfil the criteria we believe to be of primary importance. Hence evaluations have concentrated on rather modest (and easily quantifiable) aspects of these programmes' performance, such as the number of clients they serve, perceptions of their success among members of the university community, and so on. Presumably, it will be necessary to wait until universities overtly embrace the goal of promoting lifelong learning skills in students before study skills programmes, faculty development units, and the like, devote major attention to the difficult task of demonstrating their success at promoting relevant self-directed learning skills. In fact some institutions (such as those mentioned in the first part of Chapter 6) *have* adopted a deliberate philosophy of lifelong education, and in a few cases there have even been attempts to carry out systematic evaluations of the extent to which these guiding principles have been fulfilled in practice. Two cases will now be reviewed in some detail.

Goddard College. Goddard has been remarkable for its attempts over the past few decades to evaluate the success of its programmes in effecting change among students. The most ambitious study conducted by the college was a six-year experiment in curriculum organisation that took place from 1959 to 1965 supported by funds from the Ford Foundation. The research focused on three aspects of student learning at Goddard that are of particular relevance to the concerns of this book. These were students' ability to 'learn how to learn', the extent to which they developed a capacity for independent study, and their success in relating classroom learning to life outside the institution (Beecher, Chickering,

Hamlin, and Pitkin, 1966). The curriculum was oriented towards promoting student problem-solving skills and their capacity for independent study. It stressed the forging of links between the college and outside agencies and work settings, learning from peers as well as from teachers, and self-evaluation by students of their own progress in learning and development. All these goals accord well with the principles of lifelong education. Seven aspects of student development were used as criteria; these were:

- the development of competence;
- development of autonomy;
- development of identity;
- freeing of interpersonal relationships;
- development of purpose;
- management of emotions;
- development of integrity.

Change in each of these seven areas was assessed by administration of questionnaires, interviews with faculty and students, and an ambitious battery of tests and inventories. Students who entered the college in 1959 and 1960 were followed for several years, so that their progress could be monitored on a long term basis.

Although the research suffers from the lack of any control group and the fact that students entering Goddard are likely to have very special backgrounds and motivations, the richness of the longitudinal data makes the study almost unique. In brief, the findings indicate that there was consistent change over time in the development of competence and autonomy, formation of interpersonal and emotional relationships, development of integrity and identity and so on. All of these changes are consistent with the notion that the experience at Goddard facilitated the acquisition of lifelong learning attitudes and skills.

Alverno College. A somewhat similar approach was adopted in a longitudinal study of student change and cognitive development carried out at Alverno College in the early 1980s (Mentkowski and Strait, 1983). Alverno College is a small, Catholic liberal arts college for women in Milwaukee. It offers professional programmes in nursing, management, music and education, and has achieved something of a reputation for its system for assessing student competence. This is related to a specific set of learning objectives that were devised for assessing the college as a whole as well as individual programmes. An underlying theme of Alverno's curriculum is the encouragement of lifelong learning skills, promotion of the ability to transfer college learning to outside settings, and a recognition of the influence of the 'informal curriculum' on student learning and development. Great emphasis is placed upon what Alverno refers to as 'valuing', by which is meant the ability to make moral and ethical decisions (Earley, Mentkowski, and Schafer, 1980); among the other student competencies stressed by the college are communications skills, the ability to analyse and solve problems, facility in interpersonal interaction, and aesthetic understanding.

This study adopted both a cross-sectional and longitudinal approach, with over 750 students (the Alverno student body is approximately twice that size) completing a battery of instruments to measure cognitive development, skill in 'experiential' learning and other skills related to professional performance after leaving college. Sophisticated statistical procedures made it possible to account for background characteristics and programme differences, and to conclude that cognitive development and learning style were indeed affected by the college's programme. One interesting aspect of the Alverno research was that the results of the tests and measures were fed back to students on a regular basis following administration and scoring, along with advice about how to use these indicators of their performance to profit from their education and become more effective and insightful lifelong learners. This idea of using the results of research on education to facilitate the educational process itself seems as commendable as it is unusual.

The conclusions to be drawn from the Alverno and Goddard studies are sketchy. Nonetheless it can be said that there is at least some tentative evidence that the educational approaches at these colleges do indeed help to encourage lifelong learning skills. While the studies are by no means the only such research investigations that might be cited, it remains true that many of the innovations we have described have not been subjected to any detailed empirical evaluation. However, the fact that a number of the proponents of lifelong learning in higher education have indeed taken the trouble to mount complex research studies, such as those briefly described above, is an encouraging sign – especially given the fact, already mentioned, that the research evidence for the effectiveness of traditional instruction is often lacking.

A framework for evaluation

In educational evaluation, as with any other type of assessment, the process is much aided by the existence of a clear set of objectives or goals that can be used as a yardstick against which to measure the effectiveness of a particular system, approach or innovation. Both the Goddard and Alverno studies were commendable in that they began by specifying what types of effects on students their programmes might be expected to produce, given the underlying educational philosophy espoused by the college. These outcomes were then defined operationally and measures devised to determine different aspects of student learning and other changes over time. In evaluating lifelong education, then, it is important to begin by specifying appropriate evaluation criteria.

In fact we have already referred to such criteria in earlier chapters, both in terms of the outcomes we would expect in students, as well as the characteristics of educational systems and organisations. For example, to distil some of the prescriptions from earlier chapters, we have emphasised that the system of effective lifelong education should lead to:

- closer links between higher education institutions and work settings;
- emphasis upon self-directed, independent learning;
- greater flexibility in logistical and administrative arrangements in universities (for example to permit teaching and learning in different formats, at different times and in different places);
- greater cooperation between colleges and other institutions where learning occurs (e.g. museums and libraries);
- a stress on interdisciplinarity and integration of content and skills from a variety of subject areas;
- the encouragement of broad participation and greater diversity in higher education institutions, possibly linked to the decentralisation of higher education.

Teaching and learning criteria

Application of these criteria to the various educational approaches and innovations described in this book could provide a framework for the evaluation of educational practice against the criterion of lifelong

Table 7.1 *Educational approaches and teaching-learning criteria*

Criteria	Approach					
	Lectures	Guided Design	Open Learning	Cooperative Education	Personalised Instruction (PS)	Computer-Assisted Instruction
Vertical Integration						
1. Students plan their own learning	low	high	high	?	?	low
2. Students assess their own learning	low	high	?	high	low	low
3. Formative rather than summative assessment is stressed	low	high	low	?	high	low
Horizontal Integration						
1. Active rather than passive learning is stressed	low	high	low	?	high	high
2. Learning in both formal and informal settings is encouraged	low	high	low	high	low	low
3. Peer learning is encouraged	low	high	?	?	?	low
4. Students integrate material from different subject areas	low	high	?	high	low	?
5. Different learning strategies are used in different situations	low	high	?	?	low	?
6. Knowledge is used to tackle real-world problems	low	high	low	high	low	high

Table 7.1 *Continued*

Criteria	Approach					
	Lectures	Guided Design	Open Learning	Cooperative Education	Personalised Instruction (PSI)	Computer-Assisted Instruction
7. Learning process is stressed at least as much as learning content	?	high	?	?	low	?
8. Self-evaluation against real-world criteria is encouraged	low	high	?	high	low	?

education. Table 7.1 attempts to exemplify how such a framework might be constructed. Before discussing this table in more detail, it is important to stress that our interest here is not in testing the underlying principles of lifelong education which were spelled out in earlier chapters. On the contrary, these principles are adopted as basic premises for a system of higher education and, subsequently, as yardsticks against which existing systems might be judged. The intention of Table 7.2 is thus to assess a number of the approaches already discussed in terms of what we regard as some fundamental criteria for lifelong education.

The table is divided into two main parts. The first section includes criteria relating to the principle of 'vertical integration' (which stresses learning throughout the lifespan), while the second section comprises criteria that involve 'horizontal integration' (links between formal school learning and learning in other settings). On the left hand side of Table 7.1 are listed a variety of properties of teaching and learning that we have discussed in connection with the promotion of lifelong learning. These properties comprise our criteria, since they represent *a priori* desirable aspects of educational practice. For reasons of space, the number of criteria included in the table is limited, and the present list

Table 7.2 *Educational approaches and organisational criteria*

Criteria	Lectures	Guided Design	Open Learning	Cooperative Education	Personalised Instruction (PS)	Computer-Assisted Instruction
1. Broad participation of population in education (in terms of age, socio-economic class, etc.)	?	?	high	?	?	high
2. Integration of general and vocational education	low	high	?	high	low	high
3. Flexibility in curriculum/course content and organisation	low	?	low	low	low	high
4. Award of academic credit for life experiences	low	low	low	?	low	low
5. Incorporation of outside work experience into formal curriculum	low	?	low	high	low	?
6. Use of instructors who are not professional teachers	?	?	?	high	?	?
7. Development of self-instructional procedures	low	high	high	low	high	high
8. Provision of advice to students on appropriate learning skills	?	high	?	?	?	low

is intended to be illustrative rather than exhaustive. The columns of the table represent either innovations in teaching/learning that have actually been applied in higher education (such as guided design, computer-assisted instruction), or else broadly-based educational approaches (such as open learning or cooperative education). Also included is one teaching approach (the lecture) that we have argued is not supportive of lifelong learning, purely for comparison purposes.

Relating each of the approaches to the various criteria, it is possible to see in what respects they facilitate lifelong learning, and in what respects they fail to do so. We have provided, in each cell of the matrix, a rating of 'low', 'high', or 'uncertain' (indicated by a question mark). These estimates are based partly on research studies (when they are available) and partly on intuition. In most cases the question marks do not mean that it is difficult to apply the criterion in question, but that whether or not the innovation fosters lifelong learning depends upon the way it is implemented. (In fact this reservation applies to all the cells of the matrix, in the sense that it is possible to 'misapply' virtually any educational approach.)

Organisational criteria

Table 7.2 presents the same set of educational approaches in terms of selected lifelong education criteria for the *organisation* of teaching.

It is apparent that not all lifelong education principles of organisation can be easily applied to the educational practices listed, as is indicated by the presence of a question mark in the column concerned.

Further organisational criteria are listed separately below. These are not relevant to the six examples of educational practice used in Tables 7.1 and 7.2, since they are concerned with the organisation of institutions and educational structures. In fact it would be perfectly possible to develop a table that related these criteria to different types of institution or structure. However, since the focus of this book is on teaching and learning, rather than on organisation *per se*, we have not taken this analysis any further here. Relevant organisational criteria include:

- existence of overriding educational policies that encourage lifelong learning;
- provision of a diversity of higher education institutions;
- trend towards debureaucratisation of higher education;

- ease of student transfer between educational departments or 'streams';
- provision of facilities and organisational structures that encourage maximum participation in lifelong learning;
- broad participation (by students, *alumni*, etc.) in decisions affecting education and management;
- provision of necessary logistical support systems within institutions (eg: suitable classrooms, freedom from grading restrictions);
- existence of advisory services for faculty related to teaching and learning;
- encouragement of research on lifelong learning;
- encouragement of educational innovation (e.g. through development grants, relief for staff from some regular duties).

These tables and the above list provide only the bare bones of a guide to the evolution of educational practice, especially since the various lists of criteria do not go beyond the special concerns of this book. We hope, nonetheless, that they offer a basis for assessing the effectiveness of particular educational approaches from the point of view of fostering lifelong learning. Although the ratings in the cells of Tables 7.1 and 7.2 are admittedly crude, they provide some interesting insights into the various teaching and learning approaches we have discussed. In particular, it is interesting to note that innovations that look extremely promising when gauged against some of the criteria, often seem inadequate or uncertain in terms of others. It should also be remembered that although the tables might indicate that a particular learning method is almost ideally suited to promoting lifelong learning, other criteria could be taken into account that might make it seem less desirable – for instance, time involved, convenience, cost, skills and knowledge possessed by teachers. In a similar vein, the list of practical innovations could be expanded – the six depicted in the tables are merely examples. Nonetheless, we believe that the approach described here shows how the necessary evaluation could be carried out for other innovations and with an enlarged list of criteria. The construction of such an evaluative schema is an essential step in the conduct of research on lifelong education – something which is itself a prerequisite for the reform of educational practice.

Recapitulation

In the course of the present book we have emphasised two main aspects of higher education. The first involves teaching and learning skills and strategies, and the second deals with institutional and organisational characteristics. In both cases we have also attempted to spell out criteria for judging how well different educational approaches foster lifelong learning. In Tables 7.1 and 7.2 these criteria have been applied to a number of existing methods (lectures, open education, cooperative learning etc), indicating how they differ in the degree to which they foster lifelong learning. Lectures, for instance meet none of our criteria, whereas cooperative education meets many of them. (Of course this does not necessarily mean that lectures are worthless for other educational aims.) Naturally, our criteria could be used to evaluate procedures other than those we have taken here as examples – for instance, 'flexi-study', outreach programmes, or provision of developmental mentors, which are all mentioned in Chapter 3. The purpose of the exercise carried out in this chapter was not to provide an exhaustive evaluation of all possible educational approaches. Rather, we have tried to offer readers a framework for carrying out their own evaluations of approaches they might wish to adopt (whether discussed in this book or not), or which they may develop for themselves.

8 Promoting lifelong learning: some practical ideas for academics

Strategies for change

This book has attempted to develop a type of 'working philosophy' of higher education, based upon the guiding principle of lifelong learning. We have argued that lifelong education should be a major goal for universities and colleges and, to this end, have presented a critique of pedagogical and administrative practices in higher education.

Preceding chapters contain numerous instances of educational approaches that we believe are consistent with the concept of lifelong education, and in Chapter 7 we have provided criteria against which such examples might be judged. In this final chapter we turn to some practical steps that individual university teachers might take to encourage lifelong learning in their own institutions and classrooms. The suggestions given here are in many cases not especially radical, and indeed may already be used by some readers of this book. The list is not comprehensive, and the ideas are not fleshed out in detail. Rather they are intended to provide a set of examples that might stimulate instructors to consider changing their approaches to course planning, classroom teaching, and administrative practices, so as to help achieve the lifelong learning goals we believe are so important.

The ideas that follow relate to many different aspects of teaching and academic organisation. They are categorised into two broad divisions: the first group is concerned with the academic as teacher, while the second focuses on the academic as institutional decision maker. We hope that at least some of the suggestions here can provide a starting point for new instructional initiatives. Even better, we hope to inspire readers to develop their own suggestions for fostering lifelong learning in higher education.

Changes in teaching methods

For the most part, the suggestions here are all within the control of the individual teacher. They encompass the different aspects of instruction we have discussed earlier in the book – setting learning goals, choosing appropriate teaching and learning techniques, and assessing student competence or progress. For the sake of brevity, ideas are presented rather cryptically in point form, without full explication. This is partly because the suggestions hinge on approaches that have been discussed in some detail earlier in the book and also because most readers will wish to be highly selective about ideas they might try. Hence as a teacher you might do the following.

Learning goals

- Develop a set of course goals that are consistent with the principles of lifelong learning and get the help of a colleague in matching goals with student assessment tasks (exams, tests, projects) to see how the ways students are graded reflect expressed learning objectives;
- Communicate (and discuss) the learning objectives for the course with students;
- Ask students about their motives for taking the class, for example by administering a short questionnaire at the first meeting that would ask about their expectations, attitudes, needs, and goals; consider how you might modify the curriculum in the light of what you find out from the survey.

Learning and study skills

- Find out a little about how students learn, perhaps by administering one of the standard learning styles inventories (see Ramsden and Entwistle 1981, for a useful example) and discuss the results and their implications in class; be prepared to modify how you teach in the light of what you discover about student learning preferences;
- If your institution has a study skills adviser, discuss with this person what steps might be taken to help your students learn more effectively, and invite the adviser to run a session on study skills for your class;
- Ask students for study problems they encounter, and their suggested solutions, especially in the context of your assessment tasks (assignments, exams, etc.);

- Consider teaching study skills explicitly (e.g. how to write up a good lab report, how to prepare for an exam, what you expect in an essay) instead of focusing exclusively on course content;
- Teach information-finding skills as part of your course, such as conducting a search in the library, finding appropriate information sources, selecting key words that describe the issue or topic, and using relevant data bases.

Teaching methods and active learning

- Provide opportunities for active learning in the classroom, such as class projects, use of small group discussion, debates, and role playing;
- To allow more time for teaching cognitive and learning skills, disseminate course content other than by lecturing (e.g. by providing copies of course notes, audiotapes of lectures);
- Develop a self-instructional module (e.g. on audio tape, printed work-book, CAI programme) for a part of the course you find difficult to teach; make it available on a supplementary basis, and ask students to evaluate its utility;
- Try to introduce some element of peer learning, if only on a small scale – for example, make student pairs responsible for certain course topics and have them make brief class presentations;
- Use case studies and similar real-life material as a major learning activity;
- Even in a large class, try to arrange some opportunities for individual contacts between instructor, students (and, if appropriate, teaching assistants); this could range from conducting an informal 'clinic' after class to arranging a voluntary get-together at a local cafe or pub;
- Organise weekend seminars or workshops to extend or replace the officially scheduled classroom contact hours: such events can offer an excellent means of promoting self-directed and peer learning;
- Use undergraduates as teaching assistants to help run the course (e.g. to lead discussion groups), or even as research assistants on a project of relevance to the course that can later be discussed in class;
- Encourage older people to enrol in your courses, and discuss (critically if necessary) the way in which class material applies to real life, and how what is learnt in the classroom might be changed or

189

extended by incorporating examples and principles they have gathered from experience outside;

- Be willing to accept younger learners, for example those in early entrance programmes; encourage younger and older students to work together, for example on projects or in study groups;
- Get students to discover sources of information about the course material apart from traditional library resources (e.g. a museum, government office, local expert), and provide an opportunity to make use of such material in a project, essay or test;
- If appropriate, try to relate the course to some practical applications/implications in the work-place or local community, for example by a site visit or field trip;
- Emphasise the connection between the work of researchers and theorists mentioned in class and aspects of their private lives or characteristics of the society in which they lived;
- Bring practitioners into your classroom to describe the way in which theoretical knowledge can be applied, how it might be extended by knowledge of the real world, and what problems remain that new theories could help solve.

Values

- Take some time in class to discuss underlying values and ethical considerations of relevance to the course and discipline; discuss your own values with the students and explain how you came to your position; be prepared to debate such issues with students, and perhaps have them debate each other on a controversial issue of the day;
- Bring something of yourself to class by use of relevant personal examples, experiences, and anecdotes about the course material, and have students (especially older learners) describe their own experiences and attitudes.

Student assessment

- Set regular 'challenge' assignments and tests throughout the course, not necessarily for credit, and let students mark their own work; discuss answers in the light of your own solution and suggest steps for further or better work in the future;
- Have students assess one of their own assignments and/or assess the work of a fellow student (even if you retain the right to make the final decision on the grade); discuss in class the evaluation criteria

that will be used and ask for feedback on the quality of work when the assessment has been completed;
- In grading exams or assignments, give bonuses for material not taken directly from the lectures or text book;
- Give bonus marks for cross-disciplinary material and examples;
- Give higher grades for appropriate references to practical issues, such as real-life examples of theoretical points;
- Set assignment or exam questions taken from real life: for example, ask students to show how a particular aspect of theory might be applied in a real-world setting.

Instructional evaluation

- Invite a colleague to review your teaching by exchanging course outlines, assignments and exams and perhaps making a classroom visit;
- Ask students what they gained from a class or assignment by distributing a brief questionnaire that asks what ideas they have learnt can be applied in their broader lives; compare these responses with your own expectations and learning goals;
- If you have the chance, play the role of a student; for example, enrol in a correspondence course or sign up for an extension course that interests you, sit in on a class taught by a colleague at your own institution or another; consider what changes might be desirable in the course from a student's point of view; if the course is in a different, but related, discipline, think about what ideas might be used in your own classes;
- Set an assignment on a topic you know little or nothing about and do the necessary background research yourself, sharing your findings with your students;
- Carry out research on your own teaching, as writers like Patricia Cross (Cross 1986) have suggested, stressing aspects that involve lifelong learning – for example by conducting a survey of former students to see how they have utilised ideas gained from your classes;
- Document your teaching efforts and accomplishments in a 'teaching dossier' (see Shore *et al.* 1986), paying particular attention to activities related to lifelong learning, and present a summary of the dossier as part of the regular performance review; criteria for academic advancement in most universities give high priority to

teaching effectiveness, but review committees often lack convincing evidence on which to base a case.

Organisational changes affecting teaching

The suggestions given above all relate to aspects of instruction that are readily controlled by an individual teacher. But our framework for evaluation presented in Chapter 7 makes it clear that promotion of lifelong learning also requires changes in the organisation of education. In many cases such changes lie beyond the authority of members of faculty – though most universities are organised on a collegial basis, and academic staff generally have considerable say on matters of internal policies and procedures. The following suggestions all concern ways in which organisational structures might be changed to help promote lifelong learning. Once again they are presented in point form to suggest initiatives an individual teacher might take.

- Survey graduates to find out their perception of the education they have received and solicit suggestions for change in the light of their experience since leaving university;
- Survey employers to get their views on needed skills, knowledge and values; consider forming an advisory committee of employers relevant to your discipline which might act as a sounding board for proposed curriculum changes, academic standards, appropriate teaching experiences, etc;
- At the department or faculty level, examine curriculum carefully in the light of current developments in the field and the rapid expansion of knowledge; consider how much will be of relevance five years after graduation; assess how much time is spent teaching content as opposed to more generic skills; decide whether it is possible to reduce the 'seat time' required of students and substitute more independent study methods; ·
- Spend some time in class discussing with students aspects of university policy and procedure that affect them, such as grading practices, important curriculum changes, or admissions standards; consider taking back this information to the policy-making committee concerned;
- Consider introducing a course that deals exclusively with the 'process' of learning instead of the 'content' of the discipline – for

example, a course on effective problem-solving and decision-making;

● Encourage sabbaticals to develop teaching skills and/or curriculum development relevant to promotion of lifelong learning: although most sabbatical policies permit use of them for teaching-related activities, in practice there is much greater emphasis on sabbaticals to undertake research;

● If your department or institution has awards for excellent teachers, press for criteria that include encouragement of lifelong learning (instead of emphasising didactic teaching skills such as lecturing);

● If your institution has regular programme appraisals, press for attention to be paid to teaching quality as well as research output, and try to find indicators of the long-term impact of teaching programmes on the lives of students (such as the achievement of graduates);

● Work to include teaching and learning topics (e.g. on alternative teaching methods, relevance of the curriculum, etc.) as part of your academic department's or Faculty's regular colloquium series.

Matching teaching strategies to lifelong learning criteria

Each of these suggestions can be evaluated in terms of the criteria for lifelong learning spelled out in Chapter 7, and summarised in Tables 7.1 and 7.2. Naturally, some ideas meet the criteria better than others. Many represent good educational practice, but are not uniquely characteristic of lifelong learning principles. Certainly, developing course goals is a widely recommended procedure in education. However, communicating such goals to students helps meet a number of the criteria listed in Table 7.1. For instance, the idea is consistent with having students plan their own learning, with active student learning, peer learning and a stress on learning process versus course content. In the case of organisational criteria (Table 7.2), this suggestion supports the notion of course flexibility, self-instruction, and an emphasis on study skills. Similarly, arranging field trips in the local community might be said to encourage learning in informal settings, applying knowledge to tackle real-world problems (Table 7.1), use of non-professional instructors, and integration of general and vocational education (Table 7.2).

It is not necessary here to go through all suggestions and relate each one to the full list of lifelong learning criteria. Readers can easily do this for themselves. We hope, however, that as individual teachers develop their own prescriptions, they will refer to our list of criteria as a convenient yardstick for measuring appropriateness. Of course, no single proposition can fulfil all, or even most, criteria. To achieve lifelong learning requires an eclectic mixture of strategies.

Closing remarks

The most important participants in the lifelong learning process are of course the learners themselves. Research on student learning is yielding promising insights, and various programmes to improve the quality of teaching and learning, reviewed in this book, represent a useful beginning in moving higher education towards a greater emphasis on lifelong learning skills. At the same time, it remains true that in many universities and colleges teaching takes place without explicit attention being given to the learning processes that students will need not only in formal institutional learning, but in the problem solving and decision making they will encounter throughout the rest of their lives. While special programmes outside the formal curriculum may aid students in this respect, it seems essential for learning skills to be taught explicitly as part of the regular curriculum. Most university teachers have a sincere desire to see their students master not only the basic concepts of their disciplines, but to go further and apply these insights in tackling a broad range of real-world issues. However, instructors may often lack the knowledge about how best to help their students go about this vital process.

This means that, despite our repeated emphasis on student autonomy in learning, and our criticism of didactic instructional approaches, university teachers have a key role to play in fostering lifelong learning. This is especially urgent in view of the fact that many students may indeed have to *unlearn* previous study habits and attitudes to education. In particular, there will be a need to communicate new values – for example, that students' own learning is more important than blind respect for authority, that active learning is more useful than passive learning even though it may initially be more difficult. Since a great many instructors in higher education have no formal training in teaching, it will be a difficult task to move away from the prevailing didactic approaches to instructional roles that emphasise students' taking responsibility for their own learning. One encouraging factor, however, is the large numbers of university and college staff who have already demonstrated a lively interest in innovative teaching approaches that could facilitate lifelong learning skills in their students. We hope that the present book will support them in their efforts.

References

Aalbeck-Nielson, K. (1973) 'La pédagogie de la survivance. (Sur le but de l'éducation)', *Paideia*, 3, pp. 209–213.

Abercrombie, M. L. J. (1981) 'Changing basic assumptions about teaching and learning', in *Developing student autonomy in learning*, ed. D. Boud, Kogan Page, London.

Abrahamsson, K. (1986) *The need for a dialogue: On the counselling needs of presumptive adult learners in higher education* (2nd revised edition). University of Stockholm Department of Education, Stockholm.

Agoston, G. (1975) 'La communauté en tant qu'éducateur', *Acta Universitatis Szegediensis de Attila József Nominatae Sectio Paedagogica et Psychologia*, 18, pp. 5–15.

Annis, L. F. (1983) 'The processes and effects of peer tutoring', *Human Learning*, 2, pp. 39–47.

Anisef, P., Okihiro, N., and James, C. (1982) *The pursuit of equality: Evaluating and monitoring accessibility to postsecondary education in Ontario.* Ontario Ministry of Colleges and Universities.

Asian Institute of Educational Administration and Planning (1970) *Lifelong Education* (Report of a Meeting of Experts, New Delhi, August, 1970). Asian Institute of Educational Administration and Planning, Delhi.

Astin, A. W. (1977) *Four critical years: Effects of college on beliefs, attitudes and knowledge.* Jossey-Bass, San Francisco.

Aujaleu, E. (1973) 'Medicine of the future', *World Health*, April, pp. 23–29.

Barton, A. H. (1959) *Studying the effects of college education: A methodological examination of 'Changing values in college'.* Hazen Foundation, New Haven, Connecticut.

Becker, M. S., Geer, B., and Hughes, E. C. (1968) *Making the grade: The academic side of college life.* Wiley, New York.

Beecher, G., Chickering, A. W., Hamlin, W. G., and Pitkin, R. S.

(1966) *An experiment in college curriculum organisation: Report of a six-year experiment (1959–1965).* Goddard College, Plainfield, Vermont.

Beers, S. E., and Bloomingdale, J. R. (1983) 'Epistemological and instructional assumptions of college teachers.' Paper presented at the annual meeting of the American Educational Research Association, Montreal, April 1983.

Berg, B., and Ostergren, B. (1977) *Innovations and innovation processes in higher education.* National Board of Universities and Colleges, Stockholm.

Bernem, T. von. (1981) 'Motivational problems of lifelong learning', in *School and lifelong learning*, eds J. Eccleston and F. Schmidt, Landesinstitut für Curriculumentwicklung, Lehrerfortbildung und Weiterbildung, Neuss.

Beuret, G., and Webb, A. (1982) *Engineers: Servants or saviours?* Leicester Polytechnic, Leicester.

Black, J. P., Cowan, D. D., Dyck, V. A., Fenton, S. L., Knapper, C. K., and Stepien, T. M. (1988) 'Portable computers and distance education'. Paper presented at the conference of the International Council for Distance Education, Oslo, August.

Bligh, D. A. (1972) *What's the use of lectures?* Penguin, Harmondsworth, Middlesex.

Bligh, D. A. (ed.) (1982) *Professionalism and flexibility in learning.* Society for Research into Higher Education, Guildford, Surrey.

Blumenstyck, G., and Magner, D. K. (1990) 'As assessment draws new converts, backers gather to ask "What works?"', *Chronicle of Higher Education*, July 11, p. A11.

Boshier, R. (1977) 'Motivational orientations revisited: Life space motives and the Education-Participation-Scale', *Adult Education*, 27, pp. 89–115.

Botkin, J. W., Elmandjra, M., and Malitza, M. (1979) *No limits to learning.* Pergamon, Oxford.

Boud, D. (1986) *Implementing student self-assessment.* Higher Education Research and Development Association of Australasia, Kensington, New South Wales.

Boud, D. (ed.) (1988) *Developing student autonomy in learning* (2nd edn). Kogan Page, London.

Boud. D., and Falchikov, N. (1989) 'Quantitative studies of student self-assessment in higher education: A critical analysis of findings', *Higher Education*, 18, pp. 529–550.

Boud, D., Dunn, J., and Hegarty-Hazel, E. (1986) *Teaching in laboratories.*

Society for Research into Higher Education and NFER-Nelson, Guildford, Surrey.

Bouton, C., and Garth, R. Y. (1982) 'The learning group: What it is and why it may be better', *American Association for Higher Education Bulletin*, 35, 1, pp. 7–9.

Bowen, H. R. (1977) *Investment in learning: The individual and social value of American higher education*. Jossey-Bass, San Francisco.

Breathnach, A. (1983) 'University-industry cooperation in Canada', unpublished manuscript, Organisation for Economic Co-operation and Development, Paris.

Broderick, R. (1983) 'How Honeywell teaches its managers to manage', *Training*, 20, 1, pp. 18–22.

Brown, J. S., Collins, A., and Duguid, P. (1989) 'Situated cognition and the culture of learning', *Educational Researcher*, 18, 1, pp. 32–42.

Bruce, J. D., Siebert, W. M., Smullin, L. D., and Fano, R. M. (1982) *Lifelong cooperative education: Report of the Centennial Study Committee*. Massachusetts Institute of Technology, Cambridge.

Bruenig, R. H. (1980) 'Proposals for change: A study of proposals to establish development programs in five universities and one college of the California State University and Colleges', unpublished Ph.D. dissertation, Union Graduate School West.

Brzustowski, T. A. B. (1983) 'Continuing education: Requirements of the modern industrial society'. Paper presented at the Thirteenth Commonwealth Universities Congress, Birmingham, August.

Bunting, C. I. (1982) 'Looking back over a decade of innovation and alternatives', in *The test of time: Perspectives on innovation and educational improvement* (AASCU Studies, September 1982). American Association of State Colleges and Universities, Washington, DC.

Canadian Association for Adult Education (1982) *From the adult's point of view*. CAAE, Toronto.

Cahn, S. N. (1978) *Scholars who teach: The art of college teaching*. Jossey-Bass, San Francisco.

Carnegie Foundation (1972) *The fourth revolution: Instructional technology in higher education*. McGraw-Hill, New York.

Cave, M., Hanney, S., and Kogan, M. (1991) *The use of performance indicators in higher education: A critical analysis of developing practice* (2nd edition). Jessica Kingsley, London.

Centra, J.A. (1976) *Faculty development practices in U.S. colleges and universities*. Educational Testing Service, Princeton, New Jersey.

Christopulos, D., and Hafner, D. H. (1982) 'A model partnership: The

American Heart Association and higher education', in *New partnerships: Higher education and the nonprofit sector*, ed. E. M. Greenburg. New Directions for Experiential Learning, Number 18. Jossey-Bass, San Francisco.

Cohen, A. M., and Brawer, F. B. (1977) *The two-year college instructor today*. Praeger, New York.

Cohen, P. A. (1983) 'College grades and adult achievement: A meta-analysis of empirical research'. Paper presented at the annual meeting of the American Educational Research Association, Montreal, April.

Collier, K. G. (1980) 'Peer-group learning in higher education: The development of higher order skills', *Studies in Higher Education*, 5, pp. 55–62.

Collier, K. G. (ed.). (1983) *The management of peer-group learning: Syndicate methods in higher education*. Society for Research into Higher Education, Guildford, Surrey.

Cook, J. T., and Bonnett, K. R. (1981) *Mentorship: An annotated bibliography*. Far West Laboratory, San Francisco.

Coombs, P. H. (1982) 'Critical world educational issues of the next two decades', *International Review of Education*, 28, pp. 143–157.

Coombs, P. H., and Ahmed, M. (1974) *Attacking rural poverty: How nonformal education can help*. Johns Hopkins University Press, Baltimore, Maryland.

Cornwall, M. (1981) 'Putting it into practice: Promoting independent learning in a traditional institution', in *Developing student autonomy in learning*, ed. D. Boud, Kogan Page, London.

Council for National Academic Awards (1986) *The credit accumulation and transfer scheme*. CNAA, London.

Council for National Academic Awards (1988) *Assessment of prior experiential learning* (Development Services Briefing No. 4). CNAA, London.

Cropley, A. J. (1977) *Lifelong education: A psychological analysis*. Pergamon, Oxford.

Cropley, A. J. (ed.) (1979) *Lifelong education: A stocktaking*. UIE Monograph, Number 8. Unesco Institute for Education, Hamburg.

Cropley, A. J. (1980) 'Lifelong learning and systems of education: An overview', in *Towards a system of lifelong education*, ed. A. J. Cropley, Pergamon, Oxford.

Cropley, A. J. (1981) 'Lifelong learning: A rationale for teacher training', *Journal of Education for Teaching*, 7, pp. 57–69.

Cropley, A. J. (1988) 'Participation in adult education', in *International encyclopaedia of education*, eds. T. Husen and T. N. Postlethwaite, Oxford, Pergamon.

Cropley, A. J., and Dave, R. H. (1978) *Lifelong education and the training of teachers*. Pergamon, Oxford.

Cropley, A. J., and Dave, R. H. (1984) *Reforming initial and continuing education of teachers in the perspective of lifelong education.* Unpublished manuscript. Unesco Institute for Education, Hamburg.

Cropley, A. J., and Kahl, T. N. (1983) 'Distance education and distance learning: Some psychological considerations', *Distance Education*, 4, pp. 27–39.

Cross, K. P. (1980) 'Two scenarios for higher education's future', *American Association for Higher Education Bulletin*, 33. 1: 1, pp. 14–16.

Cross, K. P. (1981) *Adults as learners.* Jossey-Bass, San Francisco.

Cross, K. P. (1986) 'A proposal to improve teaching or what "taking teaching seriously" should mean', *American Association for Higher Education Bulletin*, 39, 1, pp. 9–14.

Dauber, H., and Verne, E. (eds.) (1976) *Freiheit zum Lernen.* Rowohlt, Hamburg.

Dave, R. H. (1973) *Lifelong education and school curriculum.* UIE Monograph, Number 1. Unesco Institute for Education, Hamburg.

Davis, L., and Knapp, J. (1978) *The practice of experiential education: A CAEL status report.* Council for the Advancement of Experiential Learning, Columbia, Maryland.

Dewey, J. (1938) *Experience and education.* Collier, New York.

Dickson, D. (1983) 'French students schedule mass protests to coincide with debate on reform', *Chronicle of Higher Education*, May 18, pp. 25–26.

Donne, S. L. (1983) 'The changing university: Survival in the information society', *The Futurist*, 17, 4, pp. 55–60.

Draves, B. (1981) *The free university: A model for lifelong learning.* Association Press, Chicago.

Dubin, S. S. (1974) 'The psychology of lifelong learning: New developments in the professions', *International Review of Applied Psychology*, 23, pp. 17–31.

Duke, C. (1976) *Australian perspectives in lifelong education.* Australian Council for Educational Research, Melbourne.

Dyck, V. A., Black, J. P., Cowan, D. D., and Fenton, S. L. (1988) 'The challenges of teaching computer science by distance education'.

Paper presented at the conference of the International Council for Distance Education, Oslo, August.

Earley, M., Mentkowski, M., and Schafer, J. (1980) *Valuing at Alverno: The valuing process in liberal education*. Alverno College, Milwaukee, Wisconsin.

Eccleston, J. E., and Schmidt, F. (1979) *School and lifelong learning*. Landesinstitut für Curriculumentwicklung, Neuss.

Eble, K. E. (1972) *Professors as teachers*. Jossey-Bass, San Francisco.

Educational Services and Teaching Resources Unit. (1982) *Trunk courses at Murdoch University: A report of the opinions of a sample of tutors and students*. ESTR Unit, Murdoch University, Murdoch, Western Australia.

Eide, K. (1980) 'Work, leisure, education'. Paper presented at the Seminar on Lifelong Learning and Recurrent Education, Haderslav, Denmark, May.

Elgie, K. (ed.). (1982) *The social impacts of computerisation*. Waterloo Public Interest Research Group, Waterloo.

Elton, L. (1982) 'Assessment for learning', in *Professionalism and flexibility in learning*, ed. D. A. Bligh, Society for Research into Higher Education, Guildford, Surrey.

Elton, L. (1938) 'Improving the cost-effectiveness of laboratory teaching', *Studies in Higher Education*, 8, pp. 79–85.

Environment Canada (1990) *A framework for discussion of the environment: The Green Plan, a national challenge*. Environment Canada, Ottawa.

Evans, N. (1987) *Assessing experiential learning: A review of progress and practice*. Longman (for the Further Education Unit), York.

Evans, R. I. (1968) *Resistance to innovation in higher education*. Jossey-Bass, San Francisco.

Evans, R. I., and Leppman, P. K. (1968) *Resistance to innovation in higher education: A social psychological exploration focussed on television and the establishment*. Jossey-Bass, San Francisco.

Farago, J. M. (1982) 'When they bought in, did we sell out? David Riesman on the student as consumer', *Journal of Higher Education*, 53, pp. 701–705.

Farrell, C. S. (1983) 'The computerization of Carnegie-Mellon', *Chronicle of Higher Education*, March 30, pp. 6–7.

Faure, E. (1972) (with others) *Learning to be: The world of education today and tomorrow*. Unesco and Harrap, Paris and London.

Ferrier, B., Marrin, M., and Seidman, J. (1988) 'Student autonomy in learning medicine: Some participants' experiences', in *Developing student autonomy in learning* (2nd edn), ed. D. Boud, Kogan Page, London.

Fields, C. M. (1983) 'New disputes erupt in 2 U.S. agencies over White House's civil-rights stance', *Chronicle of Higher Education*, May 14, pp. 17–18.

Finkel, D. L., and Monk, G. S. (1978) *Contexts for learning: A teacher's guide to the design of intellectual experience.* The Evergreen State College, Olympia, Washington.

Finkel, D. L., and Monk, G. S. (1979) 'The design of intellectual experience', *Journal of Experiential Education*, 2, 3, pp. 31–38.

Finniston, M. (1980) 'Lifelong learning for the professions', in *Education beyond school: Higher education for a changing context*, ed. N. Evans, Grant McIntyre, London.

Friedrich, R. J., and Michalak, S. J. (1983) 'Why doesn't research improve teaching? Some answers from a small liberal arts college', *Journal of Higher Education*, 54, pp. 158–161.

Gaff, J. G. (1978) 'Overcoming faculty resistance', in *Institutional renewal through the improvement of teaching*, ed. J. G. Gaff, New Directions for Higher Education, Number 24. Jossey-Bass, San Francisco.

Garry, A., and Cowan, J. (1986) *Continuing professional development: A learner-centred strategy.* Further Education Unit and Professional, Industrial and Commercial Updating, Stanmore, Middlesex.

Geis, G. L., and Smith, R. (1983) 'If professors are adults'. Paper presented at the annual meeting of the American Educational Research Association, Montreal, April.

Gelpi, E. (1980) 'Politics and lifelong education policies and practices', in *Towards a system of lifelong education*, ed. A. J. Cropley, Pergamon, Oxford.

Gibbs, G. (1977) 'Can students be taught how to study?', *Higher Education Bulletin*, 5, 2.

Goldschmid, M. L. (1971) 'The learning cell: An instructional innovation', *Learning and Development*, 2, 5, pp. 1–6.

Goldschmid, M. L. (1981) ' "Parrainage": Students helping each other', in *Developing student autonomy in learning*, ed. D. Boud, Kogan Page, London.

Goodlad, S. (ed.) (1982) *Study service: An examination of community service as a method of study in higher education.* National Foundation for Educational Research/Nelson, London.

Goodlad, S., Pippard, B., and Bligh, D. A. (1982) 'The curriculum of higher education', in *Professionalism and flexibility in learning*, ed. D. A.

Bligh, Society for Research into Higher Education, Guildford, Surrey.

Gow, L., and Kember, D. (1990) 'Does higher education promote independent learning?' *Higher Education*, 19, pp. 307–322.

Grant, J. A. (1971) 'Sandwich plan in England', in *Handbook of cooperative education*, ed. A. S. Knowles and Associates, Jossey-Bass, San Francisco.

Greenaway, H., and Mortimer, D. (1979) 'Britain (polytechnics): A case of rapidly evolving institutions', in *Staff development in higher education: An international review and bibliography*, ed. D. C. B. Teather, Kogan Page, London.

Gray, P. J. (1990) 'Campus profile', *Assessment Update*, 2, 3, pp. 4–5.

Greenberg, E. M. (ed.). (1982) *New partnerships: Higher education and the nonprofit sector*. New Directions for Experiential Learning, Number 18. Jossey-Bass, San Francisco.

Gregor, A. (1981) 'The professor's perception of the teaching role', *Proceedings of the Seventh International Conference on Improving University Teaching*, pp. 535–543.

Guild, A. (1982) 'Something in the air', *Times Higher Education Supplement*, September 24, p. 10.

Gustafson, K. L. (1977) 'Can you really do instructional development on two cents a day?', *Journal of Instructional Development*, 1, pp. 28–29.

Gustafson, K. L., and Bratton, B. (1983) 'Instructional improvement centers in higher education: A status survey'. Paper presented at the annual meeting of the American Educational Research Association, Montreal, April.

Harasim, L. M. (ed.) (1990) *Online education: Perspectives on a new environment*. Praeger, New York.

Harper, P. (1983) 'The working person's educator', *The Executive*, October, pp. 1–4.

Hayes, R. A., and Travis, J. H. (1974) *Employer experience with cooperative education: Analysis of costs and benefits*. Detroit Institute of Technology Cooperative Education Research Center, Detroit.

Health and Welfare Canada (1986) *Achieving health for all: A framework for health promotion*. Health and Welfare Canada, Ottawa.

Heath, D. H. (1977) 'Academic predictors of adult maturity and competence', *Journal of Higher Education*, 48, pp. 613–652.

Heerman, B., Enders, C. C., and Wine, E. (eds.) (1980) *Serving lifelong learners*. New Directions for Community Colleges, Number 29. Jossey-Bass, San Francisco.

Hefferlin, J. B. (1969) *Dynamics of academic reform*. Jossey-Bass, San Francisco.

Heffernan, J. M., Macy, F. U., and Vickers, D. F. (1976) *Educational brokering: A new service for adult learners*. National Center for Educational Brokering, Syracuse, New York.

Heller, J. I., Reif, F., and Hungate, H. N. (1983) 'Theory-based instruction in scientific problem solving'. Paper presented at the annual meeting of the American Educational Research Association, Montreal, April.

Heron, J. (1981) 'Assessment revisited', in *Developing student autonomy in learning*, ed. D. Boud, Kogan Page, London.

Hoggart, R., Stephens, M., Taylor, J., and Smethurst, R. (1982) 'Continuing education within universities and polytechnics', in *Professionalism and flexibility in learning*, ed. D. A. Bligh, Society for Research into Higher Education, Guildford, Surrey.

Horn, J. L. (1982) 'The aging of human abilities', in *Handbook of developmental psychology*, ed. B. J. Wolman, Prentice-Hall, Englewood Cliffs, New Jersey.

Houle, C. O. (1961) *The inquiring mind*. University of Wisconsin Press, Madison.

Hounsell, D. (1983) 'Improving students' learning techniques', *University of Birmingham Teaching News*, March, pp. 4–5.

Howard, A. (1986) 'College experiences and managerial performance', *Journal of Applied Psychology*, 71, pp. 530–552.

Hubermann, M. (1979) 'Live and learn: A review of recent studies in lifelong education', *Higher Education*, 8, pp. 205–215.

Hubert, G. (1989) 'Mixed mode study: Has it got a future?', *Studies in Higher Education*, 14, pp. 219–229.

Huczynski, A. (1983) *Encyclopedia of management development methods*. Gower, Aldershot.

Hummel, C. (1977) *Education today for the world of tomorrow*. Unesco, Paris.

Illich, I., and Verne, E. (19775) 'Le piège de l'école à vie', *Le Monde de l'Education*, 1, pp. 11–14.

Jacks, M. L. (1946) *Total education: A plea for synthesis*. Paul, Trench, Trubner, London.

Jacob, P. E. (1957) *Changing values in college: An exploratory study of the impact of college teaching*. Harper and Brothers, New York.

Jalling, H. (1979) 'Sweden: Strong central provision complementing local initiatives', in *Staff development in higher education: An international review and bibliography*, ed. D. C. B. Teather, Kogan Page, London.

Johnes, J., and Taylor, J. (1990) *Performance indicators in higher education: U.K. indicators*. Open University Press, Buckingham.

Jones, F. (1982) 'Taking steps to end the bias against technology', *Times Higher Education Supplement*, December 10, p. 8.

Kabel, R. L. (1983) 'Ideas for managing large classes', *Engineering Education*, 74, 2, pp. 80–83.

Karpen, U. (1980) 'Implementing lifelong education and the law', in *Towards a system of lifelong education*, ed. A. J. Cropley, Pergamon, Oxford.

Keeton, M. (1983) 'Half a loaf is not enough', *CAEL (Council for the Advancement of Experiential Learning) News*, 6, 9, pp. 2–3.

Keller, P. (1982) *Getting at the core: Curricular reform at Harvard*. Harvard University Press, Cambridge, Massachusetts.

Kloss, G. (1982) 'A suitable case for treatment', *Times Higher Education Supplement*, December 12, p. 10.

Knapper, C. K. (1980) *Evaluating instructional technology*. Croom Helm, London.

Knapper, C. K. (1984) 'Staff development in a climate of retrenchment', in *Research and Development in Higher Education, Volume 5*, ed. I. R. Dunn, Higher Education Research and Development Association of Australasia, Kensington, New South Wales.

Knapper, C. K. (1988a) *Teaching effectiveness at the University of Alberta*. University of Alberta, Edmonton.

Knapper, C. K. (1988b) 'Lifelong learning and distance education', *American Journal of Distance Education*, 1, pp. 63–72.

Knapper, C. K. (1988c) Technology and lifelong learning, in *Developing student autonomy in learning*, ed. D. Boud, Kogan Page, London.

Knapper, C. K. (1990) 'Lifelong learning and university teaching', in *Higher education in the late twentieth century: A Festschrift for Ernest Roe*, ed. I. Moses, Higher Education Research and Development Society of Australasia, Kensington, New South Wales.

Knapper, C. K., and Wills, B. L. (1983) 'Teaching computing across the curriculum: A Canadian viewpoint', in *Informatics education for all students at university level*, eds. F. B. Lovis and E. D. Tagg, North Holland Publishing, Amsterdam.

Knights, S., and McDonald, R. (1982) 'Adult learners in higher education: Some study problems and solutions from Australian experience', *British Journal of Educational Technology*, 13, pp. 237–246.

Knowles, M. S. (1970) *The modern practice of adult education: Andragogy versus pedagogy*. Association Press, New York.

Knowles, M. S. (1975) 'Non-traditional study: Issues and relations', *Adult Leadership*, 23, pp. 232–235.

Knox, A. B. (1974) 'Higher education and lifelong learning', *Journal of Research and Development in Education*, 7, pp. 13–23.

Kolb, D. A., and Fry, R. (1975) 'Towards an applied theory of experiential learning', in *Theories of group processes*, ed. C. L. Cooper, Wiley, New York.

Konrad, A. G. (1983) 'Faculty development practices in Canadian universities', *Canadian Journal of Higher Education*, 13, 2, pp. 13–25.

Kozma, R. B., Belle, L. W., and Williams, G. W. (1978) *Instructional techniques in higher education.* Educational Technology, Englewood Cliffs, New Jersey.

Kuh, G. D. (1981) *Indices of quality in the undergraduate experience.* AAHE-ERIC Higher Education Research Report, Number 4. American Association for Higher Education, Washington, D. C.

Kulich, J. (1982) 'Lifelong education and the universities: A Canadian perspective', *International Journal of Lifelong Education*, 1, pp. 123–142.

Kurland, N. D. (1980) 'Alternative financing arrangements for lifelong education', in *Towards a system of lifelong education*, ed. A. J. Cropley, Pergamon, Oxford.

Larson, C. O., Dansereau, D. F., and Goetz, E. (1983) 'Cooperative learning: The role of individual differences'. Paper presented at the annual meeting of the American Educational Research Association, Montreal, April.

Lawson, K. (1982) 'Lifelong education: Concept or policy?', *International Journal of Lifelong Education*, 1, pp. 97–108.

Lengrand, P. (1970) *An introduction to lifelong education.* Unesco, Paris.

Lengrand, P. (1986) *Areas of learning basic to lifelong education.* Pergamon, Oxford.

Leverhulme Programme of Study into the Future of Higher Education. (1983) *Excellence in diversity: Towards a new strategy for higher education.* Society for Research into Higher Education, Guildford, Surrey.

Lindquist, J. (ed.) (1978a) *Designing teaching improvement programs.* Pacific Soundings Press, Berkeley, California.

Lindquist, J. (1978b) *Strategies for change.* Pacific Soundings Press, Berkeley, California.

Lindquist, J. (ed.) (1979) *Increasing the impact of social innovations funded by grant-making organisations.* Kellogg Foundation, Battle Creek, Michigan.

Linsky, A. S., and Straus, M. A. (1975) 'Student evaluations, research productivity, and eminence of college faculty', *Journal of Higher Education*, 46, pp. 89–102.

Little, T. C. (1983) 'The institutional context for experiential learning', in *Making sponsored experiential learning standard practice*, ed. T. C. Little, New Directions for Experiential Learning, Number 20. Jossey-Bass, San Francisco.

Lockwood, T. (1982) 'What should the baccalaureate degree mean?', *Change*, 14, 8, pp. 38–44.

Long, H. B. (1974) 'Lifelong learning: Pressure for acceptance', *Journal of Research and Development in Education*, 7, pp. 2–12.

Loring, R. K. (1978) 'The continuing education universe – USA'. Paper presented at the Salzburg Seminar on Continuing Education, August 6–26.

Lynch, J. (1982) *Policy and practice in lifelong education*. Nafferton Books, Driffield, East Yorkshire.

Main, A. (1980) *Encouraging effective learning: An approach to study counselling*. Scottish Academic Press, Edinburgh.

Marriott, S. (1982) *A backstairs to a degree: Demands for an open university in late Victorian England*. Leeds Studies in Adult and Continuing Education, Leeds.

Marshall, J. (1982) 'Putting things right by degrees', *Times Higher Education Supplement*, October 24, p. 10.

Marshall, L. A., and Rowland, F. (1981) *A guide to learning independently*. Longman Cheshire, Melbourne.

Marton, F. (1983) Review of 'Student Learning in Higher Education', *Journal of Higher Education*, 54, pp. 325–331.

Marton, F., and Saljo, R. (1976a) 'On qualitative differences in learning: I – Outcome and process', *British Journal of Educational Psychology*, 46, pp. 4–11.

Marton, F., and Saljo, R. (1976b) 'On qualitative differences in learning: II – Outcome as a function of the learner's conception of the task', *British Journal of Educational Psychology*, 46, pp. 115–127.

Maslen, G. (1982) 'Part-timers' myth dispelled', *Times Higher Education Supplement*, December 24, p. 7.

Masuda, Y. (1981) *The information society as post-industrial society*. World Future Society, Washington, D.C.

Mathias, H., and Rutherford, D. (1983) 'Decisive factors affecting innovation: A case study', *Studies in Higher Education*, 8, pp. 45–55.

McCabe, R. H. (1978) *Academic-economic planning systems*. Miami-Dade Community College, Miami.

McCabe, R. H. (1982) 'Quality and the open-door community college', in *Underprepared students*, ed. K. P. Cross, Current Issues in Higher Education, Number 1, 1982–83. American Association for Higher Education, Washington, D.C.

McClusky, H. Y. (1974) 'The coming of age of lifelong learning', *Journal of Research and Development in Education*, 7, pp. 97–106.

McConnell, D. (1990) 'Case study: The educational use of computer conferencing', *Educational and Training Technology International*, 27, pp. 190–208.

McConnell, J. V. (1980) 'On becoming a student – again', Presidential address to Division Two of the American Psychological Association, Montreal, September.

McDonald, K. (1982) 'Medical schools overvalue details, need to stress skills, panel says', *Chronicle of Higher Education*, October 27, p. 3.

McDonald, R., and Knights, S. (1979) 'Returning to study: The mature-aged student', *Programmed Learning and Educational Technology*, 16, pp. 101–105.

McIlroy, J. (1987) 'Continuing education and the universities in Britain', *International Journal of Lifelong Education*, 6, pp. 27–59.

McLean, R. S. (1983) 'Ontario Ministry of Education specifies its microcomputer'. Paper presented at the Fourth Canadian Symposium on Instructional Technology, Winnipeg, October.

Mentkowski, M., and Strait, M. J. (1983) *A longitudinal study of student change in cognitive development and generic abilities in an outcome-centered liberal arts curriculum.* Alverno College, Office of Research and Evaluation, Milwaukee, Wisconsin.

McLoughlin, W. T. (1983) 'Understanding how schools fail children', *International Review of Education*, 29, pp. 59–72.

Miller, C. M. L., and Parlett, M. (1974) *Up to the mark: A study of the examination game.* Society for Research into Higher Education, London.

Milton, O. (1982) *Will that be on the final?* Charles C. Thomas, Springfield, Illinois.

Möhle, H. (1979) 'The German Democratic Republic: Staff development in a socialist setting', in *Staff development in higher education: An international review and bibliography*, Kogan Page, London.

Morgan, A. (1983) 'Theoretical aspects of project-based learning in higher education', *British Journal of Educational Technology*, 1, pp. 68–78.

Morgan, A., Taylor, E., and Gibbs, G. (1982) 'Variations in students' approaches to studying', *British Journal of Educational Technology*, 13, pp. 107–113.

Mosbacker, W. (1975) *Growth and development of cooperative education in countries outside the United States*. University of Cincinnati, Cincinnati.

Newman, J. H. (1973) *The idea of a university*. (Originally published 1852.) Westminster, Maryland: Christian Classics.

Niebuhr, H. (1982) 'Strengthening the human learning system', *Change*, 14, 8, pp. 16–21.

Nordvall, R. C. (1982) *The process of change in higher education institutions*. AAHE-ERIC Higher Education Research Report, Number 7. American Association for Higher Education, Washington, D. C.

Nuttgens, P. (1988) *What should we teach and how should we teach it? Aims and purpose of higher education*. Wildwood House, Aldershot.

O'Leary, J. (1982) 'Education by radio to start in 1984', *Times Higher Education Supplement*, August 13, p. 6.

Orpen, C. (1982) 'Student versus lecturer assessment of learning: A research note', *Higher Education*, 11, pp. 567–572.

Ostar, A. W. (1981) 'Part-time students: The new majority for the 1980s', *Chronicle of Higher Education*, October 7, p. 56.

Pascarella, E. T., Duby, P. B., Terenzini, P. T., and Iverson, B. K. (1983) 'Student-faculty relationships and freshman year intellectual and personal growth in a non-residential setting'. Paper presented at the annual meeting of the American Educational Research Association, Montreal, April.

Pask, G. (1976) 'Styles and strategies of learning', *British Journal of Educational Psychology*, 46, pp. 128–148.

Perry, W. G. (1970) *Forms of intellectual and ethical development in the college years: A scheme*. Holt, Rinehart and Winston, New York.

Pflüger, A. (1979) 'Lifelong education and adult education: Reflections on four current problem areas', in *Lifelong education: A stocktaking*, ed. A. J. Cropley, UIE Monograph, Number 8. Unesco Institute for Education, Hamburg.

Pickering, M. (1980) 'Are lab courses a waste of time?', *Chronicle of Higher Education*, February 19, p. 80.

Pineau, G. (1980) 'Organization and lifelong education', in *Towards a system of lifelong education*, ed. A. J. Cropley, Pergamon, Oxford.

Poon, L. W. (ed.). (1980) *Aging in the 1980s*, American Psychological Association, Washington, D.C.

Pucheu, R. (1974) 'La formation permanente: Idée neuve? Idée fausse?', *Esprit*, 10, pp. 321–336.

Raaheim, K., and Wankowski, J. (1981) *Helping students to learn at university.* Sigma, Bergen.

Ramsden, P. (1982) 'How academic departments influence student learning', *Higher Education Research and Development Society of Australasia News*, 4, 3, pp. 3–5.

Ramsden, P. (1983) 'Institutional variations in British students' approaches to learning and experiences of teaching', *Higher Education*, 12, pp. 691–705.

Ramsden, P., and Entwistle, N. J. (1981) 'Effects of academic departments on students' approaches to studying', *British Journal of Educational Psychology*, 51, pp. 368–383.

Resnick, L. B. (1983) 'Mathematics and science learning: A new conception', *Science*, 220, pp. 477–478.

Richmond, W. K. (1973) 'Lifelong education', *British Book News*, 8, pp. 420–427.

Rosenman, M. (1982) 'Colleges and social change: Partnerships with community-based organisations', in *New partnerships: Higher education and the nonprofit sector*, ed. E. M. Greenburg, New Directions for Experiential Learning, Number 18. Jossey-Bass, San Francisco.

Rüegg, W. (1974) 'Le role de l'université dans l'éducation permanente', *CRE-Information*, 25, 3–20.

Samson, C. E., Graue, M. E., Weinstein, T., and Walberg, H. J. (1983) 'Academic and occupational performance: A qualitative synthesis'. Paper presented at the annual meeting of the American Educational Research Association, Montreal, April.

de Sanctis, F. M. (1977) 'A victory by Italian workers: The "150 hours."', *Prospects: A Quarterly Review of Education*, 7, pp. 280–287.

Sarason, S. B., Carroll, C., Maton, K., Cohen, S., and Lorentz, E. (1977) *Human services and resource networks: Rationale, possibilities and public policy.* Jossey-Bass, San Francisco.

Sassoon, J. (1982) 'Studying outside the red brick wall', *Times Higher Education Supplement*, September 17, p. 10.

Sawhill, J. C. (1978/79) 'Lifelong learning: Scandal of the next decade?', *Change*, 10, 11, pp. 7, 80.

Schaffner, C. (1982) 'Working engineers belong in front of classes', *Process Engineering*, 52, pp. 17–19.

Schein, E. H. (1972) *Professional education.* McGraw-Hill, New York.

Schiefelbein, E. (1980) 'Planning implications of lifelong education', in *Towards a system of lifelong education*, ed. A. J. Cropley, Pergamon, Oxford.

Schlossberg, N. K. (1990) *Improving higher education environments for adults.* Jossey-Bass, San Francisco.

Scott, P. (1985) 'Higher Education: The Next 20 Years', *International Journal of Institutional Management in Higher Education*, 9, pp. 195–207.

Scully, M. G. (1982) 'Bachelor's degree a worthless credential, conference concludes', *Chronicle of Higher Education*, November 24, p. 8.

Shor, I. (1980) *Critical teaching in everyday life.* South End Press, Boston.

Shore, B. M., Foster, S. F., Knapper, C. K., Nadeau, G. G., Neill, N., and Sim, V. (1986) *The teaching dossier: A guide to its preparation and use* (Revised edition). Canadian Association of University Teachers, Ottawa.

Sikes, W. W., Schlesinger, L. E., and Seashore, C. N. (1974) *Renewing higher education from within.* Jossey-Bass, San Francisco.

Slavin, R. E. (1983) 'Meta-nonsense: Misuse of meta-analysis in educational research'. Paper presented at the annual meeting of the American Educational Research Association, Montreal, April.

Smith, W. A. S., and Stroud, M. A. (1982) 'Distance education and new communications technologies', in *Expanding learning through new communications technologies*, ed. C. K. Knapper, New Directions for Teaching and Learning, Number 9. Jossey-Bass, San Francisco.

Snyder, B. R. (1971) *The hidden curriculum.* Knopf, New York.

Solomon, P. R., Kavanaugh, R. D., Goethals, G. R., and Crider, A. (1982) 'Overcoming fragmentation in the undergraduate psychology curriculum', *Teaching of Psychology*, 9, pp. 201–205.

Somers, C. N., and Bridges, J. A. (1982) *Post-graduate success: The relationship between experiential learning programmes and liberal studies – An exploratory model.* Michigan Consortium for the Evaluation of Nontraditional Education.

Stephens, J. M. (1967) *The process of schooling: A psychological analysis.* Holt, Rinehart and Winston, New York.

Stevens, A. (1983) 'Grannies are on the march to a better life', *The Observer*, September 25, p. 5.

Stiles, L. J., and Robinson, B. (1973) 'Change in education', in *Processes and phenomena of social change*, ed. B. Zaltman, Wiley, New York.

Stock, A. K. (1979) 'Developing lifelong education: Post-school perspectives', in *Lifelong education: A stocktaking*, ed. A. J. Cropley, UIE Monograph, Number 8. Unesco Institute for Education, Hamburg.

Stone, L. J., Murphy, L. B., and Smith, H. T. (eds.). (1972) *The competent infant: Research and comment.* Basic Books, New York.

Stonier, T. (1979) 'Changes in western society: Educational implications', in *Recurrent education and lifelong learning*, eds. T. Schuller and J. Megarry, Kogan Page, London.

Suchodolski, B. (1976) 'Education between being and having', *Prospects: A Quarterly Review of Education*, 2, pp. 142–154.

Teather, D. C. B. (ed.). (1979) *Staff development in higher education: An international review and bibliography*. Kogan Page, London.

Terenzini, P. T., Pascarella, E. T., and Lorang, W. G. (1982) 'An assessment of the academic and social influences on freshman year educational outcomes', *Review of Higher Education*, 5, pp. 86–109.

Thomas, D. S., Habowsky, J. E., Doyle, R. J., and Hertzler, E. C. (1981) 'What is individualized instruction? Where is it going? An introduction', *Journal of College Science Teaching*, 11, 1, pp. 10–11.

Thompson, P., Itzin, C., and Abendstern, M. (1990) *I don't feel old: The experience of later life*. Oxford University Press, Oxford.

Thorp, A. (1981) 'Professors' perceptions of the teaching role'. Report of the University Teaching Service, University of Manitoba, Winnipeg.

Times Higher Education Supplement (1982) 'Cool Reception for Secondment', December 10, 1982, p. 2.

Times Higher Education Supplement (1983) 'Poly teaching "too didactic"', October 28, 1983, p. 2.

Tough, A. T (1971) *The adult's learning projects*. Ontario Institute for Studies in Education, Toronto.

Trotter, B. (1977) 'The teacher and the goals of the university', in *If teaching is important . . . The evaluation of instruction in higher education*, eds. C. K. Knapper, G. L. Geis, C. E. Pascal, and B. M. Shore, Clarke, Irwin, Toronto.

Trow, M. A. (1982) 'Underprepared students at public research universities', in *Underprepared students*, ed. K. P. Cross. Current Issues in Higher Education, Number 1, 1982–83, American Association for Higher Education, Washington, D.C.

Turchenko, V. (1983) 'Continuity as the cornerstone of the new paradigm of education'. Paper presented at an International Meeting of Experts on the Implementation of the Principles of Lifelong Education, Hamburg, May.

Turner, J. A. (1983) 'Drew U to issue computers to all freshmen', *Chronicle of Higher Education*, November 2, p. 3.

Unesco (1983) 'Final report of the International Meeting of Experts on the Implementation of the Principles of Lifelong Education', Unesco, Paris.

University of Waterloo Gazette (1989), 'Last changes approved for math curriculum', January 25, 1989, p. 3

Vanderhayden, K., and Brunel, L. (1977) *University at home.* Harvest House, Montreal.

Vey, E., and Novick, N. (1974) 'A consulting firm in civil engineering education: A history of four years of participation'. *Proceedings of the ASCE (American Society of Civil Engineers) Civil Engineering Conference*, 1, pp. 927–936.

Wales, C. E., and Stager, R. A. (1977) *Guided design.* West Virginia University, Morgantown, West Virginia.

Walker, W. G. (1980) 'Leadership for lifelong education: The role of educational administration', in ed. A. J. Cropley, *Towards a system of lifelong education*, Pergamon, Oxford.

Wallis, C. (1983) 'Med school, heal thyself: New studies prescribe better ways of training doctors', *Time*, May 23, pp. 40–43.

Watkins, B. T. (1977) 'A good idea or a "black eye" for education?', *Chronicle of Higher Education*, October 3, p. 5.

Watkins, D. (1984) 'Student perceptions of factors influencing tertiary learning', *Higher Education Research and Development*, 3, pp. 33–50.

Wiens, B. J. (1977) *Higher education's commitment to inservice education.* ERIC Document ED 141 528.

Williams, G. (1977) *Towards lifelong education: A new role for higher education institutions.* Unesco, Paris.

Wilson, E. K. (1966) 'The entering student: Attributes and agents of change', in *College peer groups*, eds. T. M. Newcomb and E. K. Wilson, Aldine, Chicago.

Wilson, J. W., and Lyons, E. H. (1961) *Work-study college programs: Appraisal and report of the study of cooperative education.* Harper and Brothers, New York.

Wilson, T. C. (1987) 'Pedagogical justice and student evaluation of teaching forms: A critical perspective'. Paper presented at the annual meeting of the American Educational Research Association, Washington, D.C., April.

Woodward, C. A. and Neufeld, V. (1978) *Medical education since 1960: Marching to a different drummer.* Kellogg Center for Continuing Education, East Lansing, Michigan.

Index

215